Teaching One-to-One

Teaching One-to-One

The Writing Conference

Muriel Harris
Purdue University

National Council of Teachers of English
1111 Kenyon Road, Urbana, Illinois 61801

NCTE Editorial Board: Candy Carter, Julie M. Jensen, Delores Lipscomb, John S. Mayher, Thomas Newkirk, John C. Maxwell, *ex officio,* Paul O'Dea, *ex officio*

Book Design: Tom Kovacs for TGK Design

Staff Editor: Lee Erwin

NCTE Stock Number 51884

It is the policy of NCTE in its journals and other publications to provide a forum for the open discussion of ideas concerning the content and the teaching of English and the language arts. Publicity accorded to any particular point of view does not imply endorsement by the Executive Committee, the Board of Directors, or the membership at large, except in announcements of policy where such endorsement is clearly specified.

Library of Congress Cataloging-in-Publication Data

Harris, Muriel, 1937–
   Teaching one-to-one.

   Bibliography: p.
   1. English language—Rhetoric—Study and teaching.
2. English language—Composition and exercises—Study
and teaching. 3. Tutors and tutoring. I. Title.
PE1404.H37 1986   808'.042'07   86-15308
ISBN 0-8141-5188-4

Contents

Introduction   1

1 **A Rationale for One-to-One Teaching**   3
    The Role of the Conference in Teaching Writing   5
    What Does Conference Talk Accomplish?   10
    Benefits of One-to-One Teaching   16

2 **Shapes and Purposes of the Conference**   27
    Goals of a Conference   28
    The Roles of the Teacher   35
    Conference Tasks   40
    Elements of a Conference   45
    Conference Formats   48
    Conference Scheduling   50

3 **Conference Activities**   55
    Conversational Activities   55
    Directive versus Nondirective Approaches   69
    Uses of Language and Other Forms
       of Communication   71
    Conference Problems   75

4 **Diagnosis for Teaching One-to-One**   79
    The Teacher   80
    The Student   82
    The Written Product   94

5 **Strategies for Teaching One-to-One**   105
    Strategies for Working on Rhetorical and
       Composing Skills   106
    Can Grammar Be Taught?   118
    General Strategies for Grammatical Correctness   120
    Specific Strategies for Grammatical Correctness   124

Bibliography   135

Appendix A: Conference Excerpts   143

Appendix B: Practice Activities   163

Introduction

Although we tell students that writers must clearly define for themselves a unified audience and purpose, I've had to toss overboard that good advice in writing this book because it is intended for several rather different audiences and different purposes. For one group, classroom teachers who have not used conferences very extensively but who are willing to browse through a short book on the subject, I've attempted a sales pitch to get them to try more one-to-one teaching. Since conference teaching is so obviously effective and worthwhile that the one-to-one approach sells itself, my job has been to lure these people into some elbow-to-elbow contact with students. Though in doing so I've probably glossed too lightly over the problems, difficulties, and confusions that abound when we really *meet* our students, which teachers who plunge in will discover quickly enough, by that time they'll be willing to deal with what are, in the larger perspective, minor matters.

A second audience I've kept in mind are teachers who already spend some or most of their time with their students in some form of one-to-one teaching. These people don't need any of my attempts at persuasion. That would be preaching to the converted. But these readers will be looking for tips and suggestions to widen their repertoire of conference skills. For them, I've tried to include a lot of shop talk from a lot of teachers, a sort of swapping of methods, approaches, and strategies. And I've dipped into the writing of teachers from every level, from the earliest elementary grades to the college composition level, to share a wide variety of approaches.

Yet another audience I've envisioned are tutors working or preparing to work in the tutorial setting of a writing lab. Since the degree of prior experience in teaching writing varies among tutors, I've perhaps backtracked too far for some and begun with suggestions that will seem elementary to them, but other new tutors need such help, especially since their confidence in themselves is usually much lower than it ought to be. Having worked with new tutors and heard their expressions of self-doubt ("Will I really be able to help other students?" "What if I mess up?" "What if I don't know the answer?"), I know

1

such feelings exist. I also know how unwarranted these fears are, for new tutors have been selected because they have already indicated their potential. To help them forward into seeing themselves as professionals rather than as apprentices (a connotation that hovers over the word "tutor"), I've tended throughout this book to avoid the use of the word "tutor" except in matters which might only pertain to the tutorial setting of a writing lab. Instead, I've preferred to use "teacher" or "instructor" when I mean *all* teachers and *all* tutors.

For a variety of readers of this book, then, there should be some matters of use and interest: a rationale for conference teaching, some discussion of the goals and tasks of a conference and the teacher's role in the one-to-one setting, a description of all the activities that go on when a teacher and a student talk about writing together, suggestions for the kind of diagnostic work appropriate for individualized instruction, and, finally, strategies for teaching one-to-one. To round out my discussions of these topics I've borrowed from a number of fields that can offer us help. From the literature of counselors and therapists I've included suggestions to guide us in conference strategies and goals; from the psychologists' domain of cognitive style there are insights to help us diagnose differences in writing processes and sources of writing process problems; and from cultural anthropologists and teachers of English as a second language there are analyses and discussions of cultural and language differences to help us understand the writing difficulties of the increasingly large number of non-native speakers who are appearing in our classrooms and writing labs.

Included also at the back of this book are some practice activities for tutor-training classes, though these exercises should be an interesting challenge for any teacher to consider. Some of the papers there—and suggestions and methods included in this book—have been provided by some excellent teachers willing to share both their students' writing and their own insights into conference teaching. Included in this group are Robert Child, Emily Palfrey, Sharon Powley, and Paula Wilson, fellow teachers whose help I deeply appreciate. I also owe a debt of gratitude and thanks to all the instructors and peer tutors in our Writing Lab, on whom I regularly eavesdrop. They are a never-ending source of good conference-teaching skills. And there are also the hundreds and hundreds of students whom I have worked with in our writing lab and who have managed to survive all my attempts to improve my conference abilities. Finally, my constant appreciation and thanks go to Sam, Becky, and David, my favorite individuals to confer with.

Muriel Harris

1 A Rationale for One-to-One Teaching

Conferences, opportunities for highly productive dialogues between writers and teacher-readers, are or should be an integral part of teaching writing. It is in the one-to-one setting of a conference that we can meet with writers and hear them talk about their writing. And they can also hear us talk, not about writing in the abstract, but about *their* writing. This conversation should not be viewed as merely an adjunct to group instruction, for some of the more vocal advocates of writing conferences consider the conference to be the prime method for teaching writing:

> Perhaps the most successful practice in the teaching of composition has been the regular conference to discuss the problems and progress of the individual student.
>
> —James Squire and
> Roger Applebee[1]

> We should spend nearly all of our time conferring with individual writers. That seems to be what they need most—supportive response and help with their problems in the particular piece they are working on. The writing process demands it. Discourse theory calls for it. Research on writing supports it. I don't see any way around it.
>
> —Charles Cooper[2]

> We have tried conferences for three years, and we are convinced they represent the most valuable innovation in the enrichment of the high school curriculum in English.
>
> —Janet Emig[3]

Studies of groups of teachers have turned up a similar enthusiasm. In a national survey of exemplary teachers at the elementary and secondary levels, conferences proved to be the only type of feedback during the writing process that the teachers consistently agreed was helpful.[4] And a survey of some of the students of these teachers at the secondary level showed that students found talking to their teachers during the writing process to be the best technique for helping them to write. In addition, in a study of freshman composition programs

3

around the country, conducted by Stephen Witte and others,[5] composition directors considered conferences the most successful part of their
teaching programs.

Why such interest in and enthusiastic endorsements for what some
teachers might dismiss as time-consuming or anxiety-producing conversation? Those of us who include conferences as a regular part of
our teaching know from firsthand experience how effective and even
essential the one-to-one interaction with a writer is. We tend to express
not just enthusiasm but also a bit of evangelistic fervor for such
teacher-student talk. Listen to a group of teachers asked to air their
feelings about holding conferences with student writers:

> "Why do I confer with my students? Why not? It's the best way I
> teach writing."

> "How else can you get to know students and their writing?
> Talking to a whole class is just not efficient. After reading their
> papers, I know that each one needs different kinds of help."

> "In five minutes I can tell a student so much more than I can
> write on a paper. The student can also tell me what's on his or
> her mind, and—best of all—I don't have those horrendous stacks
> of papers to grade at night."

> "Other teachers ask how I can afford to devote so much time to
> conferences. How can a writing teacher afford not to?"

> "We're dreamers or dolts if we think all of our students read
> those comments we spend so long writing on their papers. A
> few minutes of talking is far more effective in getting their
> attention."

But all is not rosy optimism. Some teachers see disadvantages or
problems:

> "How can it be done with thirty students per class, a fifty-minute
> period, and students who must disappear as soon as classes are
> over?"

> "My students need to learn from others' mistakes. And my com-
> ments may be less valid than comments from their peers."

> "What a tiresome way to proceed! I don't want to say the same
> thing over and over to each student."

> "It simply takes too much time. Besides, what happens to the
> other students while I'm meeting with one student? My class-
> room would become chaotic."

"I think I'd be uneasy with some students, especially the quiet ones. They'd probably be just as uncomfortable with me, especially if I'm trying to show a student why a paper is weak."

Any teaching method that arouses such a range of reactions among teachers deserves our attention, but the conference is particularly worthy of consideration because of its popularity and because it raises important implications for how writing should be taught.

Listing advantages and disadvantages is one way to consider the merits of conferences with student writers. Another way is to step back a bit and contemplate the role of conferences in the teaching of writing, for conferences can be—and are—a part of teaching writing to students at all levels, from kindergarten to graduate seminars, and a part of teaching writing in a variety of instructional settings. In the elementary school, frequent short meetings with first or second graders as they write can be an integral part of a language arts program (as in the Australian project described in Jan Turbill's *No Better Way to Teach Writing*).[6] In the high school, conferences can be an accompaniment to classroom instruction (as Emig describes), the primary method used in a writing workshop (see, for example, Collins and Moran),[7] or a way to individualize a classroom by using a writing lab (see Sorenson).[8] And, finally, in college, conferences can be periodic meetings in addition to classes (as described by Carnicelli),[9] the primary way to structure class instruction (see Garrison),[10] or the characteristic teaching method of writing labs that supplement writing programs (see Bamberg).[11] The conference can have a place in all formats for teaching writing, but how does it fit in and what does it accomplish?

The Role of the Conference in Teaching Writing

When we incorporate conferences into composition teaching, we are also making a number of assumptions about what writing is and what the writing teacher's role is. Talking with students as they write or prepare to write indicates that we view writing as a process of discovery in which we can help the writer learn how to shape a piece of writing as it is taking form. Moreover, since the writing teacher talks with the students and reacts as a reader, students can see that writing is primarily an act of communication in which the needs of the reader are crucial considerations. The role of the teacher in all this is to assist in the process, to help each writer move through draft after draft of the writing and focus on his or her unique questions and problems. The teacher's role is also to respond as an audience or reader, to identify problems the writer may be having, and to teach the writer strategies for moving through the writing process successfully. Let's examine each of these assumptions:

Writing as Discovery

Textbook instruction telling students to formulate a main idea, develop an outline, and then write a paper has generally been discarded as having little to do with reality. Instead, we readily acknowledge the chaos of composing with statements like "I don't know what I think until I see what I write," or Lester Fisher and Donald Murray's "The writer finds out what he has to say by writing."[12] From this perspective, the act of writing is viewed as an exploration of what it is we want to say and as a discovery of the meaning that emerges as we write. Words on the page, formed and reformed until they approximate a message the writer wishes to convey to the reader, become the written communication.

The teacher's conference role here is to encourage this exploration, to help students move through the process of discovery by talking with them, asking questions, and generally keeping up the momentum of exploration. This is especially important with writers who mistakenly think of finished papers as mere transcripts of what should have been in their heads beforehand. Such students often think—or have been taught to think—that competent writers are those who don't need to do much "scratching out." If these student writers are forced to show their rough drafts, with all the messy reality of erasures, inserts, crossed-out material, and arrows, they are prone to apologizing for their inability to "get it right the first time." Teacher help here is particularly beneficial whether it is brief conversations while walking around the room as students write or the extended conversations of writing lab tutorials in which the tutor offers positive feedback to writers unsure of where their papers are headed. A tutor in the writing lab where I spend most of my teaching time reinforces this point with a metaphor, as is evident in this excerpt from a conference transcript:

Tutor: What shall we work on today?

Student: Well, the problem is that this paper isn't coming out right. What I thought I was writing on, what the assignment said, was to talk about what a particular sport means to me—one I participate in.

Tutor: What sport did you choose?

Student: I'm on the soccer team, and last year I wrestled, but I decided to write about cross-country skiing.

Tutor: What are you going to say about cross-country skiing?

Student: That's the problem. I thought I would write about how peaceful it is to be out in the country.

Tutor: So why is that a problem?

Student: As I start describing how quiet and serene it is to be out in the woods, I keep mentioning how much effort it takes to keep going. Cross-country skiing isn't as easy as some people think. But that's not part of my thesis, that cross-country skiing takes a lot of energy, so I guess I should leave it out. But now I don't know how to explain that feeling of peacefulness without explaining how hard you have to work for it. It all fits together. It's not like just sitting down somewhere and watching the clouds roll by. That's different.

Tutor: Then you'll have to include that in your point, that the peacefulness of cross-country skiing is the kind you earn by effort. Why leave that out? Part of your point you knew beforehand, but part you discovered as you wrote. That's common. It doesn't just happen in writing. Take shopping, for example. If I want a tape of some new group's album, I go to the store with the best prices and get it. I know where I'm headed, and you would too, right?

Student: Yeah, I guess so . . .

Tutor: But if I'm thinking about upgrading my stereo system, I might need to look in several places. I might even change my mind as I go or think of some alternatives that I didn't know about beforehand, depending on what I saw and learned. That's exploratory shopping, and it's like the exploratory writing you're doing right now. You don't exactly know what you'll wind up with, but it would be a shame to toss out what you found out as you went along. So, sometimes we know where we're headed, and sometimes we learn as we go. As for me, I do a lot of exploring first in writing. So, if you're like me, you need a lot of browsing time.

And so, until there is some prose on paper, the writer may have only a general sense of what is going to emerge. When writing is truly acting as a mode of discovery, we find ideas developing and taking shape before us as words are found and ideas connect or lead to other ideas. In James Moffett's terms, the writer is moving from "inner speech" to the page, inner speech being that uncertain level or stage of consciousness where material may not be so much verbalized as verbalizable, that is, potentially available to consciousness if some stimulus directs attention there. This material is capable of being put into words because, as Moffett explains, it is language-congenial thought.[13] The stimulus can be the writer's own discovery process, but we need to realize that it can also be the gentle prodding of questions or suggestions from a teacher. Inner speech, then, is something the teacher can tap when talking with a student during a conference. "Tell me about this," or "What else comes to mind here?" are probes the teacher can use to help the student draw upon material that has not yet emerged in writing.

Writing as discovery is fun—sometimes exhilarating. It is also frustrating and messy. To acknowledge that it will take some writing to find out what the writing is going to be means that the neat, orderly sequence of attempting to write a paper in one draft is less than productive. It means that draft may have to follow draft or sentences be written and rewritten as the idea is refined and reshaped. We know what this reshaping is and can talk about it, but too often we fail to help students learn how to revise because we abandon them when they are most likely to need help. Students given back drafts to revise and then left to their own devices will, as we know too well, fall back on what they know how to do, correct spelling errors or change a word or two. In a conference, on the other hand, we can work with students, helping them do the kind of revision that good writing requires. Writers don't need to be kept company all the time, but as they advance through more complex writing tasks they need to experience the use of some revision strategies with a helper at hand. Then they can go off on their own with some sense of what should be done.

Writers also need another kind of help when revising—some support and encouragement—because the messiness of working and reworking a paper can lead to surprise and dismay as a topic falls apart or changes direction during writing. Novice writers need to learn how to persist, and they need some encouragement to do so. A teacher conferring with a student during these redrafting and revising efforts is offering all-important help and support. By comparison, responding as a grader to the finished product is far less valuable to the writer, and comes at a less useful time. When the writer is in the midst of moving through drafts, even a few minutes conversing with a teacher can be productive, encouraging the writer to rethink ideas, reinforcing the idea that multiple drafts are necessary, and providing needed encouragement to continue. As one teacher explained, "Personal attention is magic. It gets them going again when they've hit some rough spots, and it makes them want to write again. Sometimes I don't even offer any assistance. Just an acknowledgment that I sympathize helps a great deal."

Writing as Process

Like any cliché, the one that proclaims that writing teachers teach the process of writing is a tired statement in need of fresh insight. But how does a teacher teach a process? We can *talk about* processes in a somewhat theoretical way, perhaps like a lecturer describing continental drift, or we can *demonstrate* processes, like a chef in a cooking class. Or we can *participate* in processes, like a tennis pro talking with a player as they practice backhands together. The writing teacher in a conference is like a coach working with the writer through all the "-ings" of writing—thinking, planning, drafting, revising, and editing—even when these occur almost simultaneously.

The conference permits teacher and student to attend to the student's own writing and the student's own processes, which may or may not be adequate for the task. Generalities from the classroom or textbook can be brought down to the reality of a specific piece of writing. For example, we can teach the process of organization far more effectively by actually helping a student organize a draft of a paper than we can by discussing with a class ways to organize or the need for organization. Besides, abstract discussions about the need for organization are pointless and unnecessary. No student ever seriously wondered whether or not writing should be organized, and dissecting a model essay to study its organizational pattern is not the best possible help for a writer confronting several pages of paragraphs that won't fall into some logical order. What produces those pages of jumbled prose is the writer's inability to impose order on chaos. The student needs help in learning how to see what is contained in that unwieldy mass of material, to see what goes where, and to realize what's missing and what should be discarded. Going through the process of organizing with the teacher at hand is far more beneficial to the writer and more easily understood than reading or hearing generalities about organization.

Working *with* the student as writing goes on can be far more valuable than classroom discussion or any other activity that precedes or follows the actual process. As Charles Cooper explains:

> What we know about composing as a process encourages us to use response-to-writing activities. We would be naive to think we could improve a complex verbal-cognitive-experiential process like composing with pencil-and-paper, fill-in-the-blank exercises or with the pre-teaching of rhetorical and usage rules. Writers are not helped by being told in advance what to avoid. They need to write, to get immediate, supportive, helpful response to what they have written, and then to write again.[14]

Abstract lists of "dos and don'ts" issued in the classroom are not only ineffective, they are hard to keep in mind in the midst of composing and can be a source of distraction for less skilled writers. Should a writer in the midst of considering what an audience needs to know about a topic really stop to consider whether his or her sentences are also a bit wordy? Textbooks that discuss audience awareness are prone to overloading the writer with long (and sometimes incompatible) warnings:

> Ask yourself what your readers may know beforehand about your topic. Explain to your readers what they may not know.
>
> Acknowledge viewpoints that your readers may have but that you don't share.
>
> Don't bore your readers by giving them unnecessary information or even unnecessary phrases and words.

Lost in such thickets, a writer might try to keep all those bits of textbook advice in mind and find him- or herself editing phrases when he or she should be considering content.

What Does Conference Talk Accomplish?

Stimulating Independent Learning

In *No Better Way to Teach Writing,* the report of an Australian project that taught writing to first and second graders by means of conferences, Jan Turbill offers her definition of what is achieved in teacher/student conversation: "[A conference] is a talk between a teacher and a child or group of children about their work. It is time set aside for that purpose. It is an incomparable means of individualizing the teaching-learning relationship. And though in one sense it is simply 'a talk,' it is also, for the teacher, an art—chiefly the art of drawing forth ideas and fostering thinking, by asking questions."[15]

The emphasis on independent learning in Turbill's description is particularly important because some critics of conference teaching see the conference as a setting where the teacher is likely to do the student's work. Writing labs, especially those with peer tutors, often face such criticisms, and some teachers are reluctant to send students to the lab because they assume that the discussion will be one-sided, that the tutor will do the thinking for the student. This can be a pitfall, but, as Turbill says, the conversation in a student-teacher meeting is an art, and the teacher who is adept at it knows that conference talk leads students into doing their own thinking.

Asking questions is one way to help students find their own answers. Another form of help that teachers and tutors can provide is offering students the opportunity to talk about writing—to articulate problems and to explain what they are doing. This ability to talk about writing is important to students' progress as writers. Without it, they are too often unable to proceed, unable to represent to themselves the problems to be solved. "There's something wrong with my paper, but I don't know what it is" is a typical lament of less-skilled students. Asked to explain, such a student might counter with "The paper just doesn't flow," and having said that still be stuck, incapable of knowing what to do next since "flow" is some intangible quality the student often can't describe. The teacher's task here is not only to help identify actual deficiencies in papers but also to help students acquire a vocabulary that permits them to talk about their writing.

In the following conversation between a writing lab tutor and a student, we can see how the tutor's questions provide the means for the student to figure out his own answers. (The tutor is deliberately acting a bit dense here, a good tactic to help a writer realize the need to inform readers of what he or she knows.) The problem being worked on is a portion of a paper that needs some specific detail to develop its general statements. At first, only the tutor uses terms such as "specific detail" and "example" (highlighted here with italics), but as the tutorial progresses the student also begins to use similar terms— a necessary first step for revising. By the time tutor and student progress to the last sentence of the paragraph they are working on, we see that the student has acquired the words he needs to talk about his writing.

The paragraph that the tutor and student are looking at is as follows:

> The most exciting thing about being a baseball pitcher is you are always in control of the game. Your performance has a direct influence on the outcome of the game. After winning a game and knowing you produced when it counted is a great feeling.

Tutor: So what you're saying here is that the pitcher is . . . that the game is controlled by the pitcher. Is that your point?

Student: Sure. It's the pitcher who really counts. His influence . . . his performance is what counts.

Tutor: Why? I can see that that's your conclusion. But why is that so? I thought batters are important too. They make the points, the runs batted in. I guess I need some *specifics* here, something that will *show* me what you mean. Can you give me an *example?*

Student: One thing is that the pitcher is there all the time, and batters keep changing. And the pitcher can give the game away if he's not careful.

Tutor: There's a problem here. I don't know that much about baseball, so I don't know *specifically* what you mean about "giving the game away." Could you give me some *details* here? Something that would let me *see* what actually happens in a game?

Student: Something that you'd *see?*

Tutor: Sure. Good writing uses *specific detail* to help the reader get down to the *concrete* stuff, where we really begin to understand, not just the *general conclusions.*

Student: OK. So . . . ah . . . *for example* . . . in a tight situation where there are runners on base and only maybe one out, that's when the pitcher can't give the batter the wrong kind of ball, one he can connect with for a double or something.

Tutor: Great! That's the kind of *detail* that helps me understand your point. That's good. What else?

Student: Another *example?*

Tutor: Sure, if you can, or go back to that first thing you mentioned about the pitcher being on the field all the time. I didn't realize that. I mean, I know it, but I didn't realize it until you reminded me. So the pitcher . . .

Student: The guy at bat keeps changing. The pitcher, he's the one on the field tossing the ball to all the batters. He controls the ball while the batters, they come and go.

Tutor: These *details* are exactly what I need to really understand your point about being in control. Be sure to add them in your next draft. Now, what about the last sentence in the paragraph? "After winning a game and knowing you produced when it counted is a great feeling." I bet you can tell me what's missing there.

Student: You need an *example?* I guess I could be *specific.*

Tutor: *Specific* about what? What phrase could you explain with an *example?*

Student: OK. I could talk about producing when it counts. I would probably have to explain that with an *example* maybe. Yeah, so you could understand.

Promoting Interaction with Readers

The kind of talk that encourages independent learning also promotes interaction between writers and their readers, a kind of interaction that Barry Kroll, in "Some Developmental Principles for Teaching Composition," advocates as particularly beneficial to the writer in the prewriting stage.[16] Talk at this stage, explains Kroll, is vital for seeing where there are weak spots or a need for more information and for considering alternative approaches. Whether it is a teacher or a peer, the presence of the other person reminds the writer of the importance of writing from the reader's perspective. A writer who has had a chance to try out a subject on a reader can gauge the degree of interest that the subject holds and can begin to realize how much the reader may already know or how much the reader needs to know. Hesitant writers, writers who keep rejecting possible subjects for writing on the assumption that they have no value, benefit greatly from early expressions of reader interest or reaction to their plans and thoughts. As planning and drafting continue, the reader remains more vivid in the writer's mind because of their talk, and all through the drafting process reader reaction continues to be helpful to the writer learning to adjust to readers' needs.

When the teacher in a conference, rather than another writer in the class, serves as the reader reacting to the writer's developing text, there are several benefits for the student. First, the writer has an experienced reader who knows how to respond. Students can and should offer peer critiques of one another's writing, but some training time is necessary to get students to respond in useful ways. Left to their own devices, with no help in learning how to offer effective reader response, some students—influenced mostly by the need to be pleasant to fellow students—are likely to offer generalized compliments about whatever they read. "Hey, great stuff. I really enjoyed this paper" is a typical polite response. And there are other problems with student readers, as Lester

Fisher and Donald Murray remind us: "The classroom . . . often prevents the student writer from finding a sensitive reader, for some students don't read other students' writing sensitively and critically, some students can't yet understand what the writer is talking about, and some students have progressed far beyond the kind of writing and the problems faced by the writer."[17] Thomas Newkirk's study of how students and instructors differ in their evaluations of student writing suggests further limitations of peer groups in providing "a fully adequate response to a student paper."[18] Despite these problems, learning how to react more effectively is an important task for student writers, not only because other writers need the help that they can provide as readers but especially because of the value of becoming educated readers of their own texts.

Another benefit of having the instructor as a reader of the writer's text is that writers are more likely to move beyond mere word-level revisions when their readers offer nonjudgmental, useful responses. Two studies reported in Thomas Reigstad and Donald McAndrew's *Training Tutors for Writing Conferences* confirm this claim. One, by P. A. Beaumont, found that tutors who are listeners and partners, who limit evaluation, and who allow students to talk are most likely to evoke substantive revision in student writing. In the other study, A. Karliner found that when an instructor acts as an error detector and prescriber of remedies, students tend to remain passive recipients of information.[19] However, when the instructor assumes the role of a collaborator—an interested but sometimes confused reader who wants to help the writer articulate ideas more clearly—students respond by making more substantive changes in drafts. Clearly, reader response by teachers or tutors who do not pass judgment or correct errors is useful to writers during both drafting and revising.

Individualizing Learning

Teaching writing to groups presents special problems not faced by other disciplines, problems such as the variety of skill levels in any class. These differences occur partly because of individual differences among writers and partly because writing is not a set of skills that develop sequentially or neatly, from words to sentences to paragraphs and then to essays. Instead, writers jump in all at once, mixing talk with writing at an early age, writing stories before they even know what a paragraph is, constructing sentences before they know how to spell or punctuate. This happens, as Donald Murray explains, because "the writing class unlike the history class does not move from the

Revolutionary War to the War of 1812 to the Civil War; each student in the class is facing his own problems at his own pace."[20]

To make things even messier, not only do writers have different individual composing processes but different processes are used at different times. Research on composing processes has not yet given us close analyses of how such processes differ among writers or for different assignments, but we know that we do not approach all of our writing tasks in the same way. Some plans are made in our heads, some on paper; some writing follows familiar scripts, some seems amorphous and in need of models. We hear from some writers that they need to walk around and rehearse their writing before confronting a piece of paper (or computer monitor), and other writers describe the need for free-writing and brainstorming to get them going. Given this diversity, George Jensen and John DiTiberio remind us that if we advise all the students in a class to follow a single writing process, it will work for some students but not others.[21] And, while it may be useful to suggest that students try a variety of approaches, those who are confused about how to proceed may become even more confused by having options. Jensen and DiTiberio's solution to this is to develop as much as we can an understanding of how people differ and then to individualize writing instruction accordingly.

Given the diversity of students' skills and composing processes, it is hard to disagree with Judith Kollman's assessment that effective teaching in the traditional classroom structure is nearly impossible. Kollman's answer is the personal approach of the conference.[22] Working individually with a student permits us to become familiar with that student's weaknesses and strengths and with the student's uniqueness as a writer and as a person. In the company of a particular writer, we can no longer be content with doling out general prescriptions and textbook advice.

Teaching Specific Strategies

Working with individual writers also means that we are more likely to tie instruction to the particular paper and to focus on what to do next, suggesting strategies for the writer to use rather than merely identifying problems. When grading papers we are apt to write "You need to limit your topic. It's not clear what your point is," but when we sit with the writer we *ask* what the point of that particular paper is. As a result, the discussion that follows may help the writer to define the topic. Or we can ask the writer to give us a brief summary of what the paper is about, another useful strategy for helping to sharpen the focus or point of a paper. Solving problems at hand is best accomplished by finding strategies to deal with those problems, and the conference setting promotes this problem-solving approach. Teaching strategies to writers is such an integral part of conferences that chapter 5 is devoted to this subject.

Benefits of One-to-One Teaching

Having explored how conferences fit in with a process approach to writing, we now return to where we began in this chapter, considering advantages. Conferences may indeed be a natural component of teaching the writing process, but a rationale for this method of working with writers still needs to provide answers to the question "Do conferences benefit students and teachers?"

Improving Writing

In 1978 Peter Schiff summarized all the empirical evidence then available that demonstrated the effectiveness or value of conferences.[23] With so little to report, his list was far shorter than advocates would like it to be, and the situation has not improved dramatically since then. But despite the limited body of research on conferences, what is available generally supports the claim that one-to-one instruction has positive effects, though no one has yet attempted to analyze which contributing factors promote success.

In the earliest of these studies, conducted in 1971 by J. P. Shaver and D. Nuhn with fourth-, seventh-, and tenth-grade underachievers in reading and writing, the students were assigned to tutoring or control groups. Results indicate that the tutoring produced significantly greater end-of-year gains in all three grade levels, and that a greater number reached their predicted potential or better, a difference still present two years later.[24] In 1974 D. G. Sutton and D. S. Arnold studied the effectiveness of tutorial assistance in remedial writing instruction compared to the classroom lectures and discussions used for a control group. Sutton and Arnold's conclusion was that the highly individualized instructional methodology employed in the writing lab had a significantly beneficial effect upon the later English grades of the students.[25]

But not all studies show conferences as advantageous. Another study conducted in 1974, by Myrna Smith and Barbara Bretcko, which examined the effect of individual conferences on the performance of students in junior college composition courses, offers a qualified answer. The results of this study indicate that it is questionable to invest the amount of time spent in six conferences during the semester, for beyond the first two conferences students conferring with their teachers didn't learn any more than those who spent the time in class.[26] While this confirmed that some conferences are better than none, a study conducted by Judith Budz and Terry Grabar in 1976 showed a negative effect for conferences. The pre- and posttests of two groups of students, one assigned to a classroom situation and the other to half a semester of classroom instruction and half of conferences, showed that the classroom students did better than the students who spent time in tutorials.[27] (An examination of the flaws of this study can be found in Sarah Freedman and Ellen Nold's response to the Budz and Grabar article.)[28] In yet another experiment in 1976, by Mildred Fritts, which involved the use of conferences in a program of college composition, one group of freshmen had weekly fifteen-minute conferences for thirteen weeks while the control group had no conferences. As a result, the experimental group showed significantly better writing achievement than did the control group.[29]

A somewhat different population of students, in a different setting, was the focus of Allan Gates's 1977 study. For Gates's experiment, twenty-two entering freshmen deemed "marginal" were given help with reading, writing, and study skills in the college's Learning Center. When compared with a similar group who did not receive such individual help, this experimental group was significantly more successful in college in that they earned better grades, were able to complete more credit hours, and had lower overall rates of withdrawal from individual classes and from the college.[30]

The use of conferences in large composition programs has been the subject of two studies. In one, conducted by Thomas Carnicelli, the data studied were the responses of eighteen hundred students at the University of New Hampshire enrolled in a freshman English program that included weekly or biweekly conferences. All of the eighteen hundred students who wrote evaluations found conferences to be more useful than classes, and students generally preferred the privacy of the conference to class scrutiny.[31] Another study of a programmatic use of conferences, conducted in 1978 by the Los Angeles Community College District, tested the effectiveness of the Garrison method of using conferences (a method described in chapter 2 of this book) in both freshman English and remedial composition classes. The results showed that students instructed according to the Garrison method showed greater gains between pre- and posttests, with the students in remedial classes showing even more gain than did the students in the standard freshman course.[32]

Saving Time

For some teachers contemplating the use of conferences, the greatest hindrance is time. They see conferences as requiring far more time than they have available. The assumption here is that conferences are an addition to the time already spent on class instruction, paper grading, and preparation. The equation doesn't quite work that way, however, especially if we acknowledge that paper grading is neither particularly efficient nor effective. Grading papers is a way to respond to student writing, but not the only way, and therein lies the great advantage—and time savings—of conferences. On a sheer time basis, John Knapp, a teacher who uses conferences primarily for evaluation, explains that with his system of fifteen-minute conferences, he spends no more time on evaluation than he did when grading papers at home.[33] There are also the arguments, offered by Barbara Fassler, that with oral feedback more can be said than with written (because we can speak more words per minute than we can write) and that oral feedback is more efficient because of the high level of concentration maintained.[34] As a replacement for paper grading, then, conferences can reduce evaluation time, and, as discussed in the next section, offer better feedback.

There is also the possibility of replacing class instruction time with conferences. In previous pages I have argued that working with writers as they write is far more effective than class presentations of abstract concepts and lists of "don'ts." If we eliminate or reduce time spent on such lectures and discussions, even more time becomes available for conferences. Should we feel that we are robbing the class of needed instruction, we can recall Roger Garrison's reminder: a class doesn't have writing problems; only individuals have problems saying what they mean.[35] And conferences do not have to be scheduled allotments of time, fifteen or twenty minutes per student; they can be even the briefest of conversations with writers as the teacher strolls around the classroom during writing or "workshop" hours.

Providing Better Feedback

> I honestly believe that the only consistently helpful and effective evaluation of student writings comes as the two of you sit down with the piece of writing, focusing directly on what's on the page. Extraordinarily successful teachers of writing have one thing in common: they spend very little time in isolation, reading and marking papers, and a great deal of time responding and discussing student writings with the writers themselves.
>
> —Dan Kirby and Tom Liner[36]

There is a generalized and obviously deeply rooted feeling that conferences provide better evaluation, but why? Why *are* comments made by a teacher sitting elbow-to-elbow with a writer better than those written on the page? Perhaps the most important answer, from the writer's perspective, is that conference comments are clearer than those written on paper. In a study conducted by Andrew Cohen of how a group of students from the State University of New York at Binghamton handled feedback on paper from teachers, 20 percent of the students reported that they attended only sparingly or not at all to the teacher's corrections. The students appeared to have a limited repertoire of strategies for processing teacher feedback, the most popular being making a mental note of the teacher's comments. Self-rated poorer learners appeared to have an even more limited repertoire of strategies. Cohen concludes that "the results show that sometimes [teacher feedback] may be too abbreviated in nature, too general, and possibly not focused enough in the areas where learners want feedback for it to have much impact on the learners."[37] Cohen's article also provides a review of other studies of the ineffectiveness of written feedback offered by teachers. Included in the category of feedback too general to be useful are uninformative comments such as "good," "interesting," or "nice work." Though they are meant as positive reinforcement, such appraisals offer students no insights into what worked well and no information that could be applied to future writing.

In another study of students' reactions to teachers' comments on papers, Mary Hayes and Donald Daiker note that students complained that one-word or short-phrase comments, such as "unclear," "explain," or "be more specific," were the least useful they received. In response to a teacher's note that a sentence was unclear, one student responded, "I would like to know why it's unclear, because it's clear to me and it would be clear to anyone who read the story!" In response to a marginal "What?" another student told Hayes and Daiker, "Uh, hmmm. Well, let's look and find out what that question mark and that 'What?' meant. I will—I mean I can't pay too much attention to it because I really didn't know what it's all about, but ah. . . . It's in between two lines and I can't figure out which it goes to."[38] In writing labs tutors exchange similar stories of students' confused attempts to figure out teacher comments. High on my list are instances of students' interpretations of two terms in our arsenal of jargon, "focus" and "coherence." One student, asked to revise "for a tighter focus on his subject," assumed that his paper needed sharper images in the middle (similar, he thought, to the focusing area in the middle of the viewfinder in his camera). Teacher comments such as "Work on coherence" or "Try for more coherence" bring out amazing ingenuity in some students' interpreting abilities. "Maybe she wants me to sound smarter, ahh, more intelligent?" offered one student. Or "I know I write too much, and I suppose it was getting sort of incoherent, especially that technical part about how acid rain interacts with marble and stuff on statues. Maybe I'll just leave that part out."

The disheartening result of this misinterpretation, as we can see, is that when a teacher's comment is not immediately clear, students often spend considerable time and effort trying to understand it—and frequently fail. How badly they fail is evident in another of Hayes and Daiker's examples. In this case, a teacher had pointed out a fragment and written on the paper "Fragment, but it works stylistically, quite well in fact." Since the class had already worked on sentence fragments, even discussing examples of fragments that were used appropriately, the teacher would undoubtedly be startled to hear the student's interpretation, ". . . a fragment. Uh, I think it means something that—it's just—it isn't really related to the preceding sentences. It's just—it's out of place. It may be relevant, but it's just in the wrong place."[39] Of course, our terminology, if left unexplained in conferences, can be equally bewildering, but the conference presents an opportunity not only to see the blank, uncomprehending stare of a mystified student but also to ask if an explanation is needed and to explain, even if only in a few words. Writing out an explanation of a term while grading papers is far less common than offering one in speech; without the writer there, it is too easy to forget his or her confusion. With the student sitting next to us that can't happen.

Beyond the confusion of jargon and arcane terminology, there is yet another kind of confusion that results from a thoroughly graded paper. As Roger Garrison explains, when a student faces a paper pockmarked with red underlinings and "sp," "punct.," "awk.," "comma splice," "not parallel," and the like, his or her reaction is apt to be confusion: Where do I begin to improve? What should I start with? Garrison's insistence on working on one writing skill at a time in a conference is his way of avoiding this type of confusion.[40] This problem is one that I have described elsewhere as a case of more being less.[41] Too much information causes a state of information overload in which the student is unable to attend to anything because everything seems to claim his or her attention simultaneously.

In the conference, confusion can be dissipated by talk. We can ask students if they understand, and students can explain to us what they meant. Areas of misunderstanding on both sides melt away, and what might have been an adversary relationship turns into a helping one. "Why didn't that student complete the assignment?" becomes "What can I do to help her understand what the assignment is?" Even the mere use of a pleasant tone of voice softens to a suggestion what can sound on paper like a drill sergeant bellowing a command ("Split this paragraph in two!").

Feedback in a conference is not only clearer, it's quicker. Except for those teachers who heroically give up their evenings, weekends, and sometimes needed sleep and family life to get papers back quickly, most students have to wait for from several days to a week to read the teacher's comments on a graded paper. Conferences, on the other hand, permit brief meetings with writers while they are writing, short exchanges in which we can give writers immediate reactions to work-in-progress. And when we confer with writers as soon as their papers are ready for a reader, the writing is fresh in the writer's mind and the comments are still relevant. A week later writers are likely to forget what problems they had and what choices they made between alternatives. (For similar reasons an ad for a camera which instantly develops its pictures proclaims "You don't have to wait a week to see if you made a mistake.") But, then, any comments at the tail end of an effort are, as Garrison points out, far less effective than on-the-spot responses: "Working with individuals in the process of making a piece of writing is the best use of your time and energy. It is also pedagogically sound: the feedback between you and a student is kept close and recurrent. Helpful intervention in another's learning activity is a succinct definition of *teaching*."[42]

Changing the Teacher-Student Relationship

The helpful intervention that Garrison mentions is also responsible for changing students' perceptions of the writing teacher's role. Except for children in the earliest grades of elementary school who have not yet experienced the ordeal of "getting a paper back" and seeing a teacher's notations all over the page, most writers know what an English teacher is supposed to do—make colored marks on the page to highlight errors and weaknesses. By the time they get to college most freshmen fear composition teachers. The only way to overcome this fear, as Dean Memering reminds us, is through informal talk between teachers and students.[43] But there's no need to wait for college to establish a helping relationship between students and teachers. At any age when students are writing, teachers can be nearby, making suggestions, giving feedback, offering help, and showing interest. Even when evaluation includes negative comments, a teacher who accompanies them with a demonstration of personal interest in the student's improvement can reduce hostility or fear. Writing teachers who see themselves not as authority figures but as advisers, coaches, or helpers are not likely to hide behind a stack of papers to grade, and students who find teachers sitting next to them are quick to adjust their image of those teachers accordingly.

Helping Writers Critique Their Writing

Writers need to develop their self-critical powers in order to appraise their work as they progress. Without this ability to draw back from what has been written—to question its content, consider alternatives, or wonder what's missing—writers are less apt to revise in any meaningful way. Deanna Gutschow promotes the growth of this critical stance by engaging in dialogue with her students during conferences, a technique students then learn to internalize and use when writing alone. Said one of her students: "Once I started my paper, I found myself 'writing for my conference,' and trying to interpret what your questions and objections would be. . . . I'm questioning what I write much more now than I ever did before. That's really slowing me down, making me think a lot harder about what I'm trying to say." When students master this inner dialectic, they can, as Gutschow says, look "inward rather than outward for critical evaluation."[44]

Gutschow's experience with eleventh and twelfth graders suggests that they rarely know how to take this critical stance toward their writing unless shown. The conference not only illustrates and demonstrates this process, it also encourages writers to practice actually being critics, to hear themselves offering opinions. Donald Graves sees an equal need for writing conferences for young children because they too need to gain a sense of voice by first hearing themselves express ideas and opinions orally. To develop these self-critical powers Graves suggests conferences every five or ten days, conferences which don't need to be more than five to ten minutes long.[45] For writers at any age conference questions and dialogue contribute to their ability to become critics—and hence revisers—of their own work.

Notes

1. James R. Squire and Roger K. Applebee, *High School English Instruction Today: The National Study of High School English Programs* (New York: Appleton-Century-Crofts, 1968), 254.

2. Charles Cooper, "Teaching Writing by Conferencing," in *Survival through Language: The Basics and Beyond*, ed. Rita Bean, Allen Berger, and Anthony Petrosky (Pittsburgh, Pa.: School of Education, Pittsburgh Univ., 1977), 21.

3. Janet Emig, "We Are Trying Conferences," *English Journal* 49 (1960): 228.

4. Sarah W. Freedman et al., *The Role of Response in the Acquisition of Written Language*, Final Report to the National Institute of Education, 1985, NIE-G-083-0065, ED 260 407; cited in Sarah W. Freedman and Anne Marie Katz, "Pedagogical Interaction During the Composing Process: The Writing Conference," in *Writing in Real Time: Modeling Production Processes*, ed. Ann Matsuhashi (Norwood, N.J.: Ablex, forthcoming).

5. Summarized in Freedman and Katz.

6. Jan Turbill, *No Better Way to Teach Writing*, (Rosebery, N.S.W., Australia: Primary English Teaching Association, 1982).

7. James C. Collins and Charles Moran, "The Secondary-Level Writing Laboratory: A Report from the Field," in *Tutoring Writing: A Sourcebook for Writing Labs*, ed. Muriel Harris (Glenview, Ill.: Scott, Foresman, 1982), 196–204.

8. Sharon Sorenson, "The High School Writing Lab: Its Feasibility and Function," in *Tutoring Writing*, 186–95.

9. Thomas A. Carnicelli, "The Writing Conference: A One-to-One Conversation," in *Eight Approaches to Teaching Composition*, ed. Timothy Donovan and Ben McClelland (Urbana, Ill.: National Council of Teachers of English, 1980), 101–31.

10. Roger Garrison, "One-to-One: Tutorial Instruction in Freshman Composition," *New Directions for Community Colleges* 2 (1974): 55–84.

11. Betty Bamberg, "The Writing Lab and the Composition Class: A Fruitful Collaboration," in *Tutoring Writing*, 179–85.

12. Lester A. Fisher and Donald Murray, "Perhaps the Professor Should Cut Class," *College English* 35 (1973): 170.

13. James Moffett, "Writing, Inner Speech, and Meditation," in *Rhetoric and Composition*, rev. ed., ed. Richard Graves (Upper Montclair, N.J.: Boynton/Cook, 1984), 65–80.

14. Charles Cooper, "Responding to Student Writing," in *The Writing Processes of Students*, ed. W. Petty and P. J. Price (Buffalo: Dept. of Curriculum and Instruction, State Univ. of New York at Buffalo, 1975), 39.

15. Turbill, 34.

16. Barry Kroll, "Some Developmental Principles for Teaching Composition," in *Rhetoric and Composition*, rev. ed., ed. Richard Graves (Upper Montclair, N.J.: Boynton/Cook, 1984), 258–62.

17. Fisher and Murray, 169.

18. Thomas Newkirk, "Directions and Misdirections in Peer Response," *College Composition and Communication* 35 (1984): 303.

19. See Thomas J. Reigstad and Donald A. McAndrew, *Training Tutors for Writing Conferences* (Urbana, Ill.: ERIC Clearinghouse on Reading and Communication Skills and National Council of Teachers of English, 1984).

20. Donald Murray, *A Writer Teaches Writing: A Practical Method of Teaching Composition* (Boston: Houghton Mifflin, 1968), 16.

21. George H. Jensen and John K. DiTiberio, "Personality and Individual Writing Processes," *College Composition and Communication* 35 (1984): 285–300.

22. Judith Kollman, "How to Teach Composition on an Individual Basis—and Survive," *Journal of English Teaching Techniques* 8 (Summer 1975): 13–17.

23. Peter Schiff, *The Teacher-Student Writing Conference: New Approaches* (Urbana, Ill.: ERIC Clearinghouse on Reading and Communication Skills, 1978), ED 165 190.

24. J. P. Shaver and D. Nuhn, "The Effectiveness of Tutoring Underachievers in Reading and Writing," *The Journal of Educational Research* 65, no. 3 (1971): 107–12.

25. D. G. Sutton and D. S. Arnold, "The Effects of Two Methods of Compensatory Freshman English," *Research in the Teaching of English* 8 (1974): 241–49.

26. Myrna Smith and Barbara Bretcko, "Research on Individual Composition Conferences" (Urbana, Ill.: ERIC Clearinghouse on Reading and Communication Skills, 1974), ED 091 709.

27. Judith Budz and Terry Grabar, "Tutorial versus Classroom in Freshman English," *College English* 37 (1976): 654–56.

28. Sarah W. Freedman and Ellen Nold, "On Budz and Grabar's 'Tutorial versus Classroom' Study," *College English* 38 (1976): 427–29.

29. Mildred F. Fritts, "The Effects of Individual Teacher Conferences on the Writing Achievement and Self-Concept of Developmental Junior College Writing Students" (Ph.D. diss., Mississippi State, 1976), *Dissertation Abstracts International* 37 (1977): 4185A. ED 138 988.

30. Allan F. Gates, "A Study of the Effects of Work Undertaken in an Independent Learning Center by Marginal Students at Marshalltown Community College" (Ph.D. diss., Drake University, 1977), *Dissertation Abstracts International* 37 (1977): 7002A.

31. Carnicelli, 101, 105–6.

32. Cited in Jo An McGuire Simmons, "The One-to-One Method of Teaching Composition," *College Composition and Communication* 35 (1984): 228–29.

33. John V. Knapp, "Contract/Conference Evaluations of Freshman Composition," *College English* 37 (1976): 650.

34. Barbara Fassler, "The Red Pen Revisited: Teaching Composition through Student Conferences," *College Composition and Communication* 40 (1978): 186–90.

35. Quoted in Charles Dawe and Edward Dornan, instructor's manual for *One-to-One: Resources for Conference-Centered Writing*, 2d ed. (Boston: Little, Brown, 1984), iii.

36. Dan Kirby and Tom Liner, *Inside Out: Developmental Strategies for Teaching Writing* (Montclair, N.J.: Boynton/Cook, 1981), 201.

37. Andrew Cohen, "Student Processing of Feedback on Their Compositions," in *Learner Strategies: Research Directions and Educational Implications,* ed. A. Wenden and J. Rubin (London: Pergamon, forthcoming).

38. Mary F. Hayes and Donald Daiker, "Using Protocol Analysis in Evaluating Responses to Student Writing," *Freshman English News* 13, no. 2 (1984): 4.

39. Hayes and Daiker, 3.

40. Quoted in Dawe and Dornan, iii.

41. Muriel Harris, "The Overgraded Paper: Another Case of More Is Less," in *How to Handle the Paper Load, Classroom Practices in Teaching English, 1979-80,* ed. Gene Stanford (Urbana, Ill.: National Council of Teachers of English, 1979), 91-94.

42. Quoted in Dawe and Dornan, iii.

43. Dean W. Memering, "Talking to Students: Group Conferences," *College Composition and Communication* 24 (1973): 306-7.

44. Deanna Gutschow, "Stopping the March through Georgia," in *On Righting Reading, Classroom Practices in Teaching English, 1975-76,* ed. Ouida Clapp (Urbana, Ill.: National Council of Teachers of English, 1975), 100.

45. Donald Graves, *Writing: Teachers and Children at Work* (Portsmouth, N.H.: Heinemann, 1983), 649-50.

2 Shapes and Purposes of the Conference

When asked to describe a typical conference, writing lab tutors and teachers who spend most of their time working one-to-one with students can't offer easy answers. Instead, it's likely that they will describe typical characteristics of conferences: they are exhausting, the level of concentration is high, the intensity of the give-and-take can fry one's brain. Sometimes a conference ambles down several paths before finding a direction; at other times, it's difficult to define what *was* accomplished in all that talk. But whatever the direction, degree of clarity, or level of concentration, conferences are not repetitious—and it's hard to decide what might be "typical." Exact similarity isn't possible because writers are not alike. Even the same writer at different times, with different assignments, has different concerns. This doesn't imply that chaos reigns when two people meet to talk about writing. What gives shape and structure to these conversations are the goals that drive the conference forward and the strategies used to get there.

This chapter, then, is an overview, offering different perspectives on the goals, types, elements, and formats of conferences. In later chapters we will look at general plans (see chapter 3) and specific strategies (see chapter 5) to help students learn composing, revising, and editing skills, but here we are concerned neither with strategies nor with specific content but with a broader view of the goals of conferences and how to achieve them. Keeping such goals in mind is necessary because without a larger frame of reference, a conference can dissolve into a series of somewhat random responses to a student's paper. Instructors without goals in mind are especially prone to discussing whatever is most observably wrong with a paper simply because it swims into view so quickly. For undergraduates being trained as tutors, too, it is all too easy at first to plunge into the correction of spelling errors, even with a first draft.

One way to determine goals is to consider the following questions: What is the teacher's purpose—or role? What moves the conference forward, and where is it headed? What type of conference is it that the teacher and student are involved in? Is it diagnostic? Evaluative? And, because a conference proceeds through stages, what happens during the beginning, middle, and end of a conference? Such a lengthy list of considerations indicates how much is going on in a conference in addition to what is being said.

Goals of a Conference

Helping Writers Become Independent

The primary goal of a writing conference, like any other instructional method, is to make the student a skilled, knowledgeable practitioner of the field. The teacher's goal here is to work him- or herself out of a job, that is, to make the student independent. Jerome Bruner explains: "Instruction is a provisional state that has as its object to make the learner or problem solver self-sufficient. . . . The tutor must correct the learner in a fashion that eventually makes it possible for the learner to take over the corrective function himself. Otherwise, the result of instruction is to create a form of mastery that is contingent upon the perpetual presence of a teacher."[1]

We all know how passive students can be, waiting for us to tell them not just what to write about, how many pages to fill, and "what is wrong" with a paper, but also what to do to improve it. To make writers self-sufficient, able to function on their own, we have to shift the burden to them, not an easy task for students conditioned to wait for a higher authority to pass judgment on what they should do. Typically, such a student is bereft of suggestions when asked a standard opening question in a writing lab tutorial, "How can I help you?" "My teacher doesn't like my paper" is the usual reply before the student lapses into silence, waiting for the tutor to specify what must be done about this. To break the potentially unending loop of writing and waiting for directions from a teacher or tutor, such students need to learn that it is their job to ask and answer their own questions. Leading students to self-sufficiency is a difficult task that can be handled in several ways. Some teachers shift immediate and total control to the student; others choose to proceed with a stronger guiding hand, controlling the conference until students learn how to acquire independence.

At one end of this spectrum, where students are completely in charge of their own writing, is the approach described by Archibald MacLeish for "creative writing" courses devoted to the art of writing:

> The student writes. The teacher reads. And the object of the
> teacher's reading is to learn if he can how closely the knowing of
> the words approximates the knowing of their writer. It may be
> less. It may be far, far more, for such is the nature of the struggle

between a writer and the obdurate material of words in which he works. But whether less or more, the only question the man who undertakes to teach can ask is the question of the adequacy of the writing to its own intent. As a writer himself he may call it "good" or "bad." As a man he may have his human opinion of the mind which conceived it. But as a teacher of writing it is not his task to tell his students what they should try to write or to judge their work by the standards he would apply to his own or his betters'.[2]

Still leaving the ball in the student's court, Donald Murray describes his role as a teacher of writing in somewhat similar terms: "I'm really teaching my students to react to their own work in such a way that they write increasingly effective drafts. They write; they read what they've written; they talk to me about what they've read and what the reading has told them they should do."[3] Murray's approach to helping students become independent writers (illustrated in an excerpt from one of his conferences included in appendix A at the back of this book) is achieved in part by means of a set of questions to use at the beginning of a writing conference, questions designed to place the responsibility for analyzing and evaluating writing in the student's lap:

What did you learn from this piece of writing?

What do you intend to do in the next draft?

What surprised you in the draft?

Where is the piece of writing taking you?

What do you like best in the piece of writing?

What questions do you have of me?

In such a conference the writer leads and the teacher follows. "Action in conferences is redefined as intelligent *reaction*," says Donald Graves.[4] Graves lists symptoms of teachers who act rather than react: they talk more than the writer does, they ignore where the writer is in a draft, they meddle with the writer's topic, they teach skills too early in a conference, they ask questions they know the writer can't answer, and they supply words and phrases for the writer to use.

The last symptom on Graves's list is particularly evident in a conference where the teacher has forgotten the goal of helping the writer become independent. In such a conference, when the writer and teacher are concerned with a particular piece of writing, it is dangerously easy for the instructor to wade in and begin revising. The paper is there on the table while options are being discussed. If the writer falters and cannot see how to use the teacher's suggestions, possibilities will occur to the teacher for ways to rewrite a sentence or restructure a paragraph. It is tempting to share the solution the instructor has in mind, composing specific sentences for the writer or offering specific solutions that encroach on the writer's independence. Such a conversation can sound like excerpt 4 in appendix A, in which Tim proceeds to tell the student what must be done and allows the student only minimal opportunities to enter the conversation.

What is forgotten in conferences where instructors do little beyond issuing marching orders (do this, do that) is the advice offered by Lester Fisher and Donald Murray: "The teacher must remember his role and not over-teach. It is not his responsibility to correct a paper line by line, to rewrite it until it is his own writing. It is the student's responsibility to improve the paper and the teacher's responsibility to make a few suggestions which may help the student improve."[5] Important advice, but difficult to follow. Writing teachers are inclined to be service-oriented, that is, people who find it rewarding to offer help in active ways, and they also enjoy tinkering with prose. Given both propensities, the dangers of robbing students of the initiative are great. Says one teacher of her work with young children, "I find the most difficult part is resisting the adult temptation to tell a child what to do or at least make leading suggestions. With practice I now feel more confident about when to question and when to leave a problem with the child."[6] A teacher who regularly confers with young children about their writing records such a session in which she does battle with her urge to provide answers:

Steven Learns to Insert Sentences

Steven handed me his story. "For publishing," he said.
"Have you read it to a friend?" I asked.
"Yes, but he's dopey. He says it's muddled up."
"Read it to me," I said . . . It confused me too. In fact I only realised it was about a car race when he announced that "Number 10 won." So I asked him to tell me the story without looking at the words.
"Well, they were all lined up at the edge of the road—"
"Wait," I said. "Where is that part in the story?"
Irritated, he looked, then said, "I haven't wrote that yet."
"Well, where would you write it so the reader knows your story is about a car race?"
He picked up his pencil and wrote the sentence—at the end! Into my impatient mind flashed the uncharitable thought, "No, dimwit, write it at the beginning." But I managed to stay silent . . . When he finished, I asked him to read it back.
When he did so he said, "That's not right." Then reluctantly, "That sentence doesn't make sense there."

> "Do you know what you can do about it?"
> "I could write it up there"—pointing to the top of the page.
> "M-m-m, but I don't have enough room."
> "What else could you do?" I asked, dying to tell him.
> After what seemed an age, "I could draw a line to there."
> He drew a line from the sentence to the top of the page and for
> good measure wrote, "PUT HERE."[7]

While the goal of all writing teachers is to help writers become self-sufficient, not all advocates of the conference approach see themselves as "reactors" rather than "actors." In Roger Garrison's method of teaching writing by means of conferences (illustrated in an excerpt from one of his conferences in appendix A), teachers initially serve as editors, offering their experience and skills to writers somewhat like the master in a master-apprentice relationship. Teachers using Garrison's method usually meet in brief (three- to five-minute) conferences where the focus is on a single problem that the teacher and student have identified as important. Garrison's hierarchy of operational skills or concerns begins with content, checking for adequate ideas and information. If there is no problem here, the teacher moves down to the second category, tone. Here the teacher-as-editor looks for purpose, persona, and audience. If the tone displays no need of immediate attention, the teacher moves on to check organization, then style (including diction and syntax), and finally mechanics (grammar and punctuation). Having read the paper and talked with the student, the teacher first diagnoses the major problem that needs attention and then offers suggestions for what can be done to solve it. The teacher's guidance is more overt here than in conferences such as Murray's, which proceed by questions for students to answer.

Using Garrison's approach as his framework, Thomas Carnicelli defines six tasks of the conference teacher:[8]

to read the paper carefully

to offer encouragement

to ask the right questions that get the student actively involved

to evaluate the paper

to make specific suggestions for revision

to listen to the student

While the teacher acts as an editor, evaluating and suggesting revisions, the student still has an active role in this type of conference. Thomas Reigstad and Donald McAndrew, who also use Garrison's structure for the conference, remind us that the writer, not the tutor or teacher, still does the actual revising. The instructor is viewed here as a trained assistant who suggests strategies for the writer to experiment with, but the writer is the one who applies those strategies to the writing. The teacher's job is to monitor and guide. Reigstad and McAndrew follow Garrison's hierarchy, structuring the conference so that "higher order concerns" of thesis or focus, appropriate voice or tone, organization, and development take precedence over "lower order concerns" of sentence structure, punctuation, usage, and spelling.[9]

Instructors who choose to lead students toward self-sufficiency by serving as editors need not follow Garrison's hierarchy. They can begin with the rhetorical components of subject, purpose, and audience, helping students identify and formulate topics they are working on, the purpose for which the paper is being written, and the audience to whom it is addressed. Once these are clearly articulated in the writer's mind, in notes, or in the draft of the paper under consideration, the instructor can move on to other rhetorical matters such as organization, clarity, and coherence. When these do not need to be discussed, the instructor and student can move on to stylistic concerns such as conciseness and word choice, and finally to editing concerns such as grammatical correctness and spelling.

Instructors who work from any of these sets of priorities have as their goal helping the writer achieve competence in specific skills, skills observable in the written product. Instructors can also focus their attention on processes writers are using as they write. Goals are then defined from a slightly different vantage point, to help the student become a competent planner, transcriber, and reviser, and discussion in the conference is more likely to be concerned with planning or inventing strategies, methods for revising, and so on. This doesn't eliminate or bypass attention to the particular paper the writer is concerned with, but writing or revising that paper is not the focus of discussion. As Stephen North says, in defining the role of the writing center, "Our job is to produce better writers, not better writing."[10] When a student appears in a writing lab after having gotten a graded paper back, the instructor's purpose is to help that student prepare for further writing.

Motivating Writers

While guiding writers toward independence, instructors can also pursue another goal, helping their students want to become good writers who care about their own writing. Students who come to realize that writing is important will—we fervently hope—strive for their own improvement rather than for mere grade satisfaction. In the classroom, teachers can create a climate where writing is seen as important and where good writing can be illustrated and discussed. But this process becomes personalized for students only in the conference, where their own strengths are discussed and where they can get immediate feedback on their improvement. Reinforcement and positive comments offered in the conference are also effective because they are delivered in person and offered in greater detail. Including some emphasis on the good points of a paper keeps students from focusing only on its negative qualities, a habit conditioned by years of getting papers back with what Judith Kollman calls "gotchas" running down the margins of their papers.[11] Even when weaknesses are pointed out in a conference, comments tend to be less harsh, more humanized, when extended in a conversation between people rather than transmitted in red on paper.

When a writer can meet in conferences with an instructor who demonstrates that he or she cares about the student's writing, the student is likely to agonize a bit longer over the next draft before bringing it to the reader. Instructors who recognize this sometimes have to put aside attempts to make progress with specific writing skills so that they can concentrate on providing the student with some motivation to continue.

Attending to the Writer's Concerns

Whether we invite the student to answer our questions (e.g., What problems did you have? Where are you going next?) or to attend to our hierarchy of concerns (e.g., subject, purpose, audience), we have to realize that writers also come to sessions seeking help, feedback, answers to questions, or even reassurance—matters that are on their mental agenda and therefore require attention. We cannot proceed in one direction when the student is only waiting for a lull in order to turn the conversation down a different path. Our success in achieving our goals is likely to increase in direct proportion to our ability to recognize the student's goals. (See chapter 3 for a discussion of how to listen actively to what students try to tell us.) The problem is that teachers who steep themselves in all the current discussion of what constitutes good writing and what defines a good writer will come to the conference primed and ready to discuss composing strategies, cohesion, audience awareness, or whatever else teachers value. Yet nowhere in our literature have we polled student writers about what they value, what constitutes—in their terms—"good writing." Some students come to conferences seeking ways to get a better match between the sentences on the page and the not yet clearly articulated thoughts in their minds; they are unhappy because "it doesn't say what I wanted it to say." Other goals among student writers are producing a piece of prose that is "different" or "interesting" or producing a paper that "flows." If we deal only with what's available on the page, we won't realize these problems exist in the student's mind. Qualities such as "being different" or "interesting" might not rank as high on our priority list as clarity, coherence, or adequate development, but when students desperately want such qualities in their writing (and the intensity of their desires is sometimes surprising), their concerns must be attended to. If they are not, students grow ever more cynical and more likely to view "good writing" as merely a matter of giving teachers what they want.

We should also confront the reality that another major goal for students is completing the writing assignment. From our perspective we see that writing skills must be developed over a semester or through a series of exposures to writing exercises, but students tend to be a bit more shortsighted, to see a specific assignment as a unique event, a hurdle to get over. At some point or other, if the conference discussion does not seem applicable to the paper due next Wednesday, students are likely to feel frustrated, confused, or uneasy, and to tune us out. When this happens, they stop participating in the conversation, waiting for an opportunity to ask, "But how should I write the conclusion for the paper?" or "How many pages should it be?" For a teacher dedicated to weaning students to independence, it will seem like total defeat to capitulate to such requests. But such questions can also be an invitation to broach the subject of the writer's need to make such decisions. A somewhat different approach to this, used particularly by writing lab tutors, is known as "doing a quick and dirty" in order to secure the writer's willingness to return to more important problems. That is, if the highest priority on the student's agenda is "Does this paper have any comma splices? My teacher takes off a letter grade for comma splices," the tutor may choose first to focus only on comma splices in the hope that the student, having cleared that concern from the list and having seen that he or she is in the company of someone who can really help, will be ready to move on to more important problems.

Meshing teacher goals with student goals is indeed delicate, especially when the student may be working from a storehouse of advice and instruction from previous teachers. Too many students' heads are a welter of rigid rules and confused or misperceived notions, beguiling their attention away from more important matters and toward rules they think they remember: "Don't use 'I' "; "Don't start sentences with 'but' or 'because' "; "Write with a lot of adjectives," and so on.[12] It is difficult indeed to accomplish our purposes when students are too tightly focused on inappropriate ones. But we have achieved a great deal when we finally mesh our goals with those of our students.

The Roles of the Teacher

As Coach

When we ask what hat a teacher wears in a conference, we soon discover that teachers and tutors have a whole wardrobe of hats to put on, and that they may need to change hats every few minutes. From one viewpoint, the teacher or tutor is a coach helping writers develop their own skills. The crucial distinction here is that the teacher is *not* the player but the person who stands at the sidelines watching and helping—not stepping in to make the field goal or sink the putt when the player is in trouble. Thus, typical comments of a teacher-as-coach might be:

> "You've done a good job of using specific details in this first paragraph. Can you do the same thing again in your second and third paragraphs?"

> "That sentence is hard for me to read because it's so long. I need some pause markers to help me see the different parts. Punctuation would help. Where could you add some punctuation?"

> "Last time we talked about the need for connecting words between sentences. Try to use the same techniques with this paragraph."

> "I agree. Writing a conclusion to a description can be very difficult. What possibilities have you thought of so far? Even if they aren't the greatest, let's use what you've got as starters."

Like coaches in other fields, instructors use these comments to help writers identify what they have to watch out for, what they have to work harder on, what has been working well for them, and what to build on. Beginning teachers and student tutors have perhaps the greatest difficulty with this role because it is so easy for them to forget that they are not wearing the writer's hat.

As Commentator

Elsewhere I have also described other roles of the conference teacher as commentator and counselor.[13] The commentator's role, like that of the "background" person in sportscasting, is to give a larger perspective on what's going on. In the seemingly amorphous setting of the conference, where all the student may be aware of is that there are two people talking, students can all too easily lose perspective. The teacher-as-commentator needs to help the student see how and when the discussion is moving forward and, in connecting to larger perspectives, how all of it is related to the student's growth or improvement in writing skills. At some point in a conference, a teacher-as-commentator might say to the student, "Now you've found the subject you really wanted to write about. Good job! The first draft was a great help in accomplishing that because now you are ready to move forward. You've learned something important about what first drafts can accomplish."

From another perspective, the teacher-as-commentator can help a student see what is really happening. For example, a student who has finally discovered the focus or topic of a paper can all too easily sink into feelings of defeat and announce, "But I don't know how I'd organize that kind of paper." What this student doesn't see is that he or she is not mired in quicksand but instead progressing to the next level of concern, organization. The teacher-as-commentator also draws on past experience and current knowledge to offer the kind of commentary that assures students that they are not oddballs, misfits, or inadequate writers when they experience problems. When students confess that they "just can't get it right the first time," we can assure them that they are merely experiencing the usual messiness of drafting and revising.

As Counselor

Like other counselors, teachers in writing conferences also look at the whole person, not merely the perpetrator of fragments or rambling paragraphs. To move beyond the observable errors on the page, it's necessary to inquire into the writer's previous experience, prior learning, motivation, outside problems, attitudes, and composing processes in order to form an adequate picture of how to proceed. We can see the teacher-as-counselor at work even in the following brief exchange, recorded by David Taylor, between tutor and student in a writing lab:[14]

> *Student:* I'm gonna flunk English 100. The teacher gives me an F on a paper and tells me to write it again. I write it again and get another F.
>
> *Teacher:* You really seem frustrated. You turn in a paper and you are simply told to write it again.
>
> *Student:* I don't mind writing it again. It's not knowing what he wants.

In this interchange, the tutor, using the counseling technique Taylor calls "paraphrasing" or restating what the student has just said (14), encourages the student to probe a bit deeper into what is causing the problem. Sometimes it takes a bit more "reflecting" or restating before the problem emerges so that the teacher or tutor can deal with it. In another writing lab conversation the student reveals a difficulty that might have continued to plague her if she hadn't finally aired her problem to me:

Instructor: You don't seem to have gotten very far on your paper yet. What kind of problems are you having with it?

Student: Well, I . . . you see . . . It's a difficult assignment. I spent some time with it yesterday . . .

Instructor: Have you gotten anything on paper yet that we can start with?

Student: No, I tossed everything.

Instructor: You didn't like any part of what you had written?

Student: No, it just didn't work.

Instructor: Could you tell me what you didn't like or what caused you to throw everything out?

Student: I didn't throw much out because I couldn't get going. That's the problem. It's that first introductory part. I'll be all right as soon as I get past that. I need help with an introduction.

Instructor: Why was the introduction so difficult? Your last paper started with that great story about how you got lost driving through New Mexico.

Student: Sure, I finally came up with that, and I was OK. I know you have to start with something that will catch the reader's interest. I had an English teacher a couple of years ago who said the opening sentences are the most important part of your paper. Without a knockout beginning, you lose the reader. It's so hard, but once I get past that first paragraph . . .

Instructor: Have you ever thought about writing your first paragraph later, after you've gotten the rest of the paper in shape? For some people, that's a big help. I usually just get anything down, just to get myself going, and I rework the opening later.

Student: Really? That sure would be a whole lot easier . . .

As counselors, we have to remember that we don't know until we ask—or spend some time in listening for—what might be derailing the student's efforts to write. Motivational problems ("I'm going to repair computers when I'm done with school, so why do I need to worry about spelling?"), difficulties with other school subjects, learning or physical disabilities that may have gone unheeded, or any of a number of other causes can stifle a writer's progress. Only in a conference can we consider the writer as a whole person.

As Listener

Equally important is the role of the listener. In "The Listening Eye: Reflections on the Writing Conference," Donald Murray describes the changes in what is being listened to as a paper progresses.[15] At first, in prewriting conferences, the teacher asks about students' lives and what they know. The teacher here is a friendly listener, interested in each student as an individual, a person who may have something to say. As student drafts develop, the teacher becomes a fellow writer who shares writing problems as the need occurs to focus, to shape, and to form a piece of writing. Finally, as meaning is found, the teacher becomes a reader more interested in the language of the paper. The teacher at this stage is listening closely to what the paper says. Throughout this sequence, Murray cautions, we must listen closely to hear what the student needs to know.

The changing roles of the teacher are described somewhat differently by Dan Kirby and Tom Liner in *Inside Out: Developmental Strategies for Teaching Writing*,[16] though they too stress the need to cast off certain roles as the writer develops. At the fluency stage, say Kirby and Liner, the writer needs attention, encouragement, and support. Responding at this stage means seeing potential, drawing the writer out, spotting future topics, learning more about the writer, and pointing to things that work in the writing. As the student gains confidence and gains a sense of personal voice, worrying less about getting words on paper, the teacher's role changes gradually to that of a supportive editor, one whose goal is to help writers express as powerfully and effectively as possible what they have to say. Advice is offered on a take-it-or-leave-it basis. With confident writers, the teacher's role is that of the critic, arguing fine points of diction, asking for a more consistent point of view, and challenging the writer to rework the piece.

As Diagnostician

Another role of the teacher, that of diagnostician, is particularly important in Garrison's approach, in which the teacher's role of editor is a defining characteristic in the conference Thomas Reigstad describes as "teacher-centered." This type of conference is characterized by the teacher's doing most of the talking and much of the work, reading drafts and issuing directives for specific revisions. The teacher's role is as expert, rule-giver, initiator, evaluator, interested reader, and partner in writing. In the following conference, recorded by David Taylor, the teacher begins with the student's concern and then does the work of diagnosing and defining the problem:

> *Instructor:* Ummm, this is quite pretty in places. I mean in a good way. Very gentle. How do you like it?
>
> *Michelle:* I don't know. I had a problem. At times it, well, it just doesn't, I don't know, didn't flow.
>
> *Instructor:* So you didn't think the sentences went together very well?
>
> *Michelle:* No, it's not that. It's hard to explain, but the words just weren't the right ones.
>
> *Instructor:* I see. Can you point to a spot where you had that problem? It's hard to, I know, but if—
>
> *Michelle:* (interrupting) Here where I say "happy, secure." (turns pages) "Aura of serenity." Those words just don't . . . I don't know (shakes her head).
>
> *Instructor:* I think I know what you mean. And we even have a phrase for it: "Show, don't tell." All those adjectives were trying to talk but just can't very well. Remember when we did the ladder of abstraction in class? A beautiful place—a hideaway—a hideaway in the Bahamas—a palm tree beach of white sands in the Bahamas? You just need to pick a "for instance" that will bring you down that ladder.[17]

In contrast to this kind of conference, in which the teacher leads, Reigstad offers two other models, the collaborative conference and the student-centered conference. In the collaborative conference the teacher moves in and out of the teacher-student relationship, drawing the student out, probing, asking questions, engaging in exploratory conversation, and leaving final decisions to the student. In the student-centered conference, as typified by Donald Murray's sessions, the student does most of the talking and most of the work. The student even

determines the direction of the conference, while the teacher listens
and asks questions.

An inherent danger in the teacher-centered conference, as already
mentioned, is the possibility that the teacher can unwittingly assume
total control, wresting from the student all responsibility for what
happens and closing off all avenues for student participation. (The
ratio of teacher talk to student talk in such a conference is inordinately
high.) When this happens, chances for students to improve their writing decrease dramatically. In a study of the relationship between the
nature of teacher-student interactions in a selected group of conferences and the kinds of writing which resulted from the conferences,
Suzanne Jacobs and Adela Karliner found that students need to have
equal responsibility in selecting topics for discussion if any progress
is to result. If students do some of the topic selection, explain Jacobs
and Karliner, they are forced to generate their own thoughts on the
subject, resulting in a significant change in the cognitive level of the
revision as opposed to the mere patching of a rough draft.[18] The
conclusion here is that students who sit passively in a conference are
not likely to do a turnabout and actively engage in any substantive
revision. Forced to sit still, they will continue to engage in the least
possible motion or effort. But students new to the conference setting
or students conditioned to surrender total control to teachers in the
classroom may be hesitant to leap in and make judgments, introduce
topics, and so on. Another role for the teacher then is that of an
activator, helping these students back into the driver's seat—and back
on the road to self-sufficiency.

Conference Tasks

On the way to improving students' writing, teachers have several
different kinds of tasks to accomplish in conferences. They need to get
to know their students, to do some diagnostic work, and to offer some
instruction. Unlike writing lab tutors, classroom teachers may also
have to do some evaluation. Some conferences are taken up with only
one task, perhaps a long "getting-to-know-you" session; other conferences can include some diagnostic work and some instruction. Like
the back and forth of writing, conference talk can also move forward
with some instruction and then pause to go back to some additional
diagnostic work. Later in the semester or year, evaluation can loom
large, while getting-acquainted talk is limited to a few brief exchanges
to reestablish friendly lines of communication.

Getting-Acquainted Time

Early conferences need to focus on getting acquainted, on breaking the ice so that future interaction is informal and comfortable. This is also a good time for learning students' interests and skills, information useful in helping students locate potential subjects for writing. During this time it is also important for teachers to establish their receptiveness to what students say, for, as Lester Fisher and Donald Murray remind us, most students don't believe that they have anything worth saying or, if they did, that anyone would listen.[19]

This getting-acquainted time is a time to talk as people interested in each other. Judith Kollman particularly values this because, as she explains, "Above all, the conference exists to communicate my interest in, and respect for, the individual human being with whom I am talking."[20] At the ends of conferences, as part of this interchange, Kollman often asks for criticism of the class and finds that she hears the most constructive criticism she has ever received. And an added benefit she notices is that her classroom is more relaxed and the students are less apprehensive about the teacher and more confident about the value of their own ideas.

Getting-to-know-you time includes some diagnostic work as well, because as teachers learn more about their students useful and important information can emerge. Is the student generally apprehensive about writing? Is the student's seemingly bland writing smoothing over some personal trauma? Could spelling errors be the result of reading problems? In some writing labs, other personal information is routinely gathered in questionnaires, on composing profiles, or in conversation.[21] In any conference, sympathetic listening is needed— and so is a light touch or bit of humor, which dissolves the invisible wall between teacher and student. Because this getting-acquainted time can be so enjoyable, some teachers and tutors cut it short with a guilty start, as if enjoyment and instruction were mutually exclusive. But it is hard to proceed with a successful conference without making human connections and without establishing the individuality of the person with whom we are sitting.

Diagnostic Time

When we first meet a student, we cannot proceed until we assess that student's needs or problems. In *The Writing Laboratory*, Joyce Steward and Mary Croft explain that for some students this diagnostic work in itself may be enough to direct the writer to appropriate self-improvement simply by revealing problems and clarifying acceptable ways to deal with them.[22] For example, a student who thinks he or she is unable to write a particular paper may need to realize that the real problem is a failure to understand the assignment. All such a student needs is a clearer sense of what the task is. More usually, though, diagnostic work is not the solution, but merely preparation for moving forward, and at any moment in the conversation, given some new understanding of a writer's problem, either the writer or the teacher (or both) may need to stop and reconsider the initial diagnosis. What seemed, at first, to be a student's inability to generate more arguments for a paper may really be confusion about who its audience is. Or what appears to be a punctuation problem may be an inability to recognize sentence parts. In chapter 4 we will look more closely at such intricacies of diagnosis, but the zigzagging progress of the conference is particularly evident when either writer or reader realizes that one problem may be masking another, more basic one. And, as a writer progresses through a paper or a semester, new problems become evident and more diagnosis is needed. Though diagnosis comes up again and again, however, it is particularly appropriate near the beginning of a conference or series of conferences, to set the agenda.

Instructional Time

The major portion of any conference, of course, is devoted to some kind of instruction, though this is not always obvious to students. Writers working out answers to questions such as those posed by Donald Murray earlier in this chapter may be unaware of the instructional value of what they are doing. And some instructional time is spent, as Steward and Croft point out, in problem-solving tasks such as understanding the assignment, finding ideas, selecting information, narrowing a topic, finding methods of organizing, and so on (48).

Other instructional tasks focus on skills to be acquired. Spelling, sentence structure, punctuation, usage, coherence devices, paragraphing, and other topics are writing skills to be mastered in conferences either because the writer has not succeeded in learning these matters in class or from textbooks or because the teacher thinks it's better to learn such skills in the context of the paper being written. When teachers choose the conference as the place to work on such skills, their task is twofold. First, they have to help the student recognize the problem, and then they have to help the student acquire the particular skill needed to solve it. The first task may seem at odds with paper grading, for much of what is noted in the margins of a paper eliminates the student's need to recognize errors. The underlying assumption of paper grading is that after students are shown their errors, they can check their handbooks, learn the rules, and cease forever to commit those errors. Future writing will show whether they have indeed mastered the skills. In conferences, however, we can proceed differently. We can help students learn to identify an error and then watch as they move through the rest of the text, checking for similar problems.

For some students, one conference is not enough to learn how to overcome errors resistant to quick instruction, errors such as fragments or verb tense endings. Therefore some conferences are devoted to ongoing instruction, a program or list of skills to work on that forms the agenda for as many meetings as the student needs. Writing labs, which offer a convenient facility for this kind of ongoing tutorial help, often provide it as a supplement to classroom instruction.

Evaluation Time

While evaluation in the classroom is primarily concerned with paper grading, Sarah W. Freedman's studies of the conference have led her to conclude that several types of evaluation occur during the conference: (1) teachers guide students to evaluate their own writing, (2) teachers and students evaluate the student's writing process as well as the written product, and (3) teachers give substantive, formative evaluation throughout the writing process as well as summative evaluation or grades once the product is complete.[23] Whether evaluation is offered during the course of the writing or when the paper is finished, there is a choice to make concerning whether to read the paper before meeting the student in the conference. Some teachers find great merit—and benefit—in doing the evaluation with the student present because the student gets a more immediate, fresh reader response: enjoyment, puzzled rereadings, and spontaneous comments. Whatever happens in this unrehearsed setting, writers have the opportunity to witness readers reading their prose. On the other hand, some teachers choose to read the paper beforehand so that they can offer the student the results of their reading as a prepared and considered response.

But whether or not comments are prepared in advance, the evaluation that replaces paper grading is not just an oral version of what would have been written on the page. As Nancy Sommers has observed, when we grade papers at home, it is harder to shift our focus from the paper in front of us (the product) to the process. Talking about strategies is easier in person. The result is different evaluative feedback, for as Sommers says, "What one has to say about the process is different from what one has to say about the product."[24] Product evaluation, concludes Sommers, tends to focus on mechanical issues. In Winifred Harris's study of the grading habits of thirty-six high school English teachers, she found that 66 percent of the corrections and annotations made on themes were devoted to mechanics and usage. Teachers looked at sentence structure primarily in terms of technical correctness rather than looking for the rhetorical effectiveness of variety in structural elements or kinds of sentence patterns.[25] Oral comments can also slide into mere correcting of mechanics, but with writers sitting next to us it is easier to remember to respond to the whole piece of writing rather than to two comma splices.

Oral comments not only tend to move beyond matters of mechanical correctness, they also tend to be fuller, simply because we can say more than we can write in a given amount of time. The added time and the needs of a possibly perplexed student next to us also make us more likely to speak English (instead of reverting to the mystifying written code of "awk," "ww," or "punct") and to explain difficult rhetorical concepts in a human—and humane—way.

In "The Red Pen Revisited" Barbara Fassler points out that oral comments also let the student in on the evaluation process.[26] As we read aloud and comment, the secret of how teachers assess papers becomes knowable and the reader's response to a paper becomes more vivid. If a teacher has a question, the student is there to answer or explain. When the teacher bogs down in a rambling sentence or unclear construction, the student can see that confusion really does result from such problems. Still more advantages of the evaluation conference, as pointed out by Michael Blenski, Jr., are that the student can see the close attention the teacher gives to details of the writing and that the student can also listen to the paper if the teacher reads it aloud, hearing such matters as repetitious sentence patterns or abrupt jumps between paragraphs. For those teachers who worry that students will forget their comments, Blenski suggests that they provide a written summary of a paper's strengths and weaknesses at the end of the conference.[27]

The underlying rationale of the evaluation conference, that students profit from evaluative responses, is not, however, a self-evident statement that all teachers agree with. In "Teaching the Other Self," for example, Donald Murray maintains that the effective conference teacher does not deal in praise or criticism, because all texts can be improved. Instead, the instructor discusses with students what is working in their papers and what can be made to work better, as well as what isn't working and how it might be made to work.[28] An added benefit, one familiar to writing lab tutors, is that when the tension of being judged is removed students see the teacher as a true helper or coach and therefore engage more actively in thinking about, arguing with, and revising what the teacher or tutor has suggested. In a conference where the teacher evaluates the paper, however, students are likely to adopt the "give-'em-what-they-want" approach and accept whatever statements or suggestions are made.

An alternative is to shift the burden of instruction to the student, as Donald Murray often does when he asks students what they like best about the paper and what they think needs changing. It then becomes the writer's job to be the editor and to view the paper critically. Even teachers who see themselves as the ones to offer the major editorial suggestions can begin by asking students for their own comments or by suggesting that the student read the paper aloud so that both teacher and writer can hear it. As some writers read aloud, they tend to editorialize ("That sentence was too long," "That's not exactly what I meant there," and so on), to note grammatical errors or usage problems ("I guess I need a comma there" or "That verb should be 'was caught,' not 'catches,' because I've been writing in the past"), and sometimes to note possibilities for revision ("This paragraph wasn't too clear. I should add something more about why I was so unhappy").

Elements of a Conference

One way to analyze a conference is to identify possible stages—how a conference proceeds through time from beginning to end. Even a brief glance at the conference excerpts at the end of this book will illustrate that reality is much muddier, that actual conferences do not progress neatly from one stage to the next. But if we tease out the various strands that are often intertwined, we can see a general progression from initial contact to wrapping up what has been accomplished.

At the beginning of a conference, getting acquainted or reestablishing contact takes priority as student and teacher settle in. The next stage is to do some stocktaking, to consider what is to be done. This may mean some diagnostic work to assess what the student needs: reading the paper the student has brought in, asking questions to locate difficulties, or requesting that the student identify what concerns are to be dealt with. When the particular goals for that session have been formulated, the teacher's next task is to decide on a teaching strategy. Will they discuss the topic in order to help the student formulate it more clearly? Will they do some exercises together to help the student learn how to combine sentences? Will they plunge into a brainstorming session to help the student try a strategy for developing more material? Will the forward motion be determined by the student's questions?

When the direction has been determined, the next step may be to focus the session for the student, to explain (if needed) how it will proceed. If a student is feeling bewildered, not knowing where the conference is headed or what is getting done, he or she can feel lost in what is perceived to be an amorphous or directionless conversation. "We just talked, I guess, I don't know. Whenever I said something that seemed to interest him, we talked about that some more," is one student's description of a brainstorming session she had in our writing lab. With no explanation, no attempt to help her see that the instructor had decided that this approach would help her get started, the student had no framework for understanding what had happened. Even worse, it is unlikely that she could articulate for herself the value of brainstorming as an invention strategy.

The conference can next progress through its instructional goal— practicing sentences, finding better details, suggesting revisions, and so on—and then end with some closure that explains to the student what has been accomplished and what's left to do. Even the briefest exchange as the teacher walks around a classroom may need some conclusion identifying for the student what to do next. Without that, one teacher explained to me, her junior high students were prone to calling her back to their desks as they constructed each new sentence.

Because the conference is also the primary setting in which other professionals like counselors, social workers, and therapists work, there is an extensive literature on conferences which writing teachers are beginning to tap—with some caveats. Therapists are more likely to see their clients as "disabled," a condition that need not apply to writers. The writing conference may establish a helping relationship, but there is not, as in the therapist's meeting, the need to help all clients back on their feet. Some we merely keep company with as they march along. The goal of the writing teacher is instructional, not therapeutic.

Nevertheless, teachers can borrow techniques and insights from therapists' literature, as does David Taylor in "A Counseling Approach to Writing Conferences."[29] Taylor suggests that we borrow from the counselor's world the conditions for helping relationships in conferences:

1. *The creation of an atmosphere of acceptance and trust:* The client should feel that he or she can express feelings and attitudes freely without threat of condemnation.

2. *An openness about goals:* It is necessary to make clear what the roles of the teacher and student are and what responsibility the student is to take on. This can take the form of stating, "Today we'll do X, but not Y." This helps the student focus on what the conference is meant to accomplish. This also involves being open about the purpose of a question. Instead of "What's the meaning of this paragraph?" the teacher or tutor ought to explain, "I'm confused about the point of this paragraph, about how all the information ties together as it should. What is the paragraph's main idea?" Such an explanation reveals the purpose of the question and reduces its threat.

3. *"I" language:* When we use "I" to express value statements about writing, students should then be able to see that what is said is not an unalterable axiom but one particular teacher's own ideals and reactions. "I" is also a way to react to writing in a non-threatening way. *"You* are inconsistent in your use of tenses" implies a negative judgment of the writer as well as the writing. "I" language, however, allows the teacher to reflect the reality of the situation. "I read this sentence but I don't feel I understand exactly what it is saying," or "When the tenses of the verbs in this paragraph change, I get confused" are statements that reduce the threat to the student.

Rosemary Arbur, in "The Student-Teacher Conference," also borrows from an analysis of social workers' interviews to offer seven elements of a conference:[30]

1. *Engagement:* the initial act of putting the student at ease, conveying an acceptance of the student, and identifying the purpose of the meeting

2. *Problem Exploration:* the act of leading the student from a sense that "everything" is "wrong" with the paper to a focus on what specific problems should be worked on

3. *Problem Identification:* the process of isolating as specifically as possible the most serious problem at hand

4. *Agreement to Work on a Problem Together:* the acknowledgment of a shared commitment to cooperate and to work together

5. *Task Assignment:* an articulation of what the student must do to satisfy the terms of the agreement

6. *Solution:* the stage reached when the problem is eliminated

7. *Termination:* the end of the meeting

Arbur's linear progression of elements recognizes the need for mutual consent in a conference, but it seems to relegate the instructional focus to the interval between task assignment and solution. When emphasis is given to instructional content in analyzing the conference, different elements surface. Such an analysis was done on tutorial dialogues to see how they might guide the construction of programmed tutorials on computers,[31] and the elements that emerged were as follows:

1. *Topic Selection:* Tutors appear to select topics mostly in order of importance within a framework of topic and subtopic. When a subtopic is exhausted, the tutor then pops back up to the previous topic.

2. *Questioning:* Rather than the expected sequence of presenting information and then asking about it, the tutors whose dialogues were studied exhibited an intricate interweaving of question and presentation tied to the structure of the topic selected.

3. *Review:* Tutors accomplish this through reiteration, systematic passes through the same material, and review questions about material covered earlier.

4. *Response to Error:* When tutors confronted errors made by students, the tutors exhibited several different strategies. If the student confused similar things, tutors typically pointed out the confusion and provided distinguishing characteristics that would help the student sort things out. Another procedure was to ask a question about the wrong answer that would help the student remember the right one. Finally, tutors also gave the student the right answer.

These elements, which formed the basis for the tutorial structure of the computer program SCHOLAR, are those which can be programmed. In a teacher-student conference the range is much broader, as we shall see in the discussion of conference strategies in chapter 3.

Conference Formats

Incorporating conferences into the teaching of writing is, as Charles Cooper reminds us, a radical curriculum change that costs nothing.[32] Conferences require no new facilities, equipment, or schedule changes, because they can be included in a conventional classroom, conventionally equipped. Students need only pencil and paper and a place to write, while teachers need a place to sit and talk to students about their writing. Suggestions for classroom formats are offered in the instructor's manual for Charles Dawe and Edward Dornan's *One-to-One: Resources for Conference-Centered Writing,*[33] a useful textbook for the conference-centered classroom. The format Dan Kirby and Tom Liner prefer is the writing workshop, getting groups together whenever it is helpful and holding numerous thirty-second conferences with working writers as the teacher walks around the room. Roger Garrison, whose work has been particularly influential in shifting teachers' interest toward the conference-centered classroom, specifically recommends short conferences. After the first week or so, he suggests that class meetings be abolished as the classroom becomes a writing workshop where the teacher holds conferences in one corner of the room while the students sit and write.

Another format, used in several high schools in Buffalo and described by Nina Luban, Ann Matsuhashi, and Tom Reigstad,[34] is a separate facility, a Writing Place, which is an adjunct to a writing program. These writing places offer drop-in tutorial help outside the regular classroom. In the Australian project with first and second graders described in Turbill's *No Better Way to Write,* the teacher walks around the room while the children write, conferring briefly here and there.

In *A Writer Teaches Writing* Donald Murray describes the setting he prefers, a lab where students can work and where the teacher can do his or her work—which is to encourage students individually.[35] The ideal writing lab, for Murray, should have a desk for each student and an office for the teacher, which should be a place with some degree of "acoustical privacy" and a view of the classroom, a place to which the teacher can withdraw with a student and go over a paper and where teacher and student can be candid without being heard by the rest of the class.

Murray's description is an ideal, but most of us don't work in ideal settings, and it's more likely that the teacher and students are all crowded in one classroom with no private retreat area for teacher and writer. While privacy isn't crucial, it is vital to have a setting which is not confrontational, that is, which does not place the student across from the teacher, but in a side-by-side arrangement. Best of all, as Donald Graves recommends,[36] are conferences at round tables where the slight curve enables us to see the writing comfortably. In an advocacy setting, the teacher can sit close to the writer (not opposite), can engage the writer visually (rather than avoiding eye contact), and can keep the paper in front of the writer (instead of appropriating it by holding it).

The writing lab can function as a supplement to a writing program or a place where credit courses are offered, either open-ended
and self-paced or scheduled like other courses at particular times. The
diversity of the writing lab setting, as evident in articles in the *Writing
Lab Newsletter* and the *Writing Center Journal* and in descriptions
of writing centers in the *1984 Writing Lab Directory*, includes the
standard conference formats: scheduled appointments, drop-in times,
writing rooms where tutors are available as needed, and small-group
meetings. Privacy in this setting is even rarer than in the classroom.

Conference Scheduling

The question of when to hold conferences has a simple answer—all
through the semester. If conferences are held only occasionally, they
can be offered at any time during the student's progress in writing a
paper. As Thomas Carnicelli reminds us, the conference approach is
most effective when we work with the whole writing process, helping
students as they proceed.[37] Prewriting conferences can help students
search for topics; conferences focusing on early drafts can help those
students who are off-course or have reached a dead end by suggesting questions to consider or new possibilities to explore; and conferences any time before the final draft can help with problems or offer
reader feedback. The only stage Carnicelli does not recommend—and
any seasoned conference teacher will immediately (and vehemently)
concur—is a conference after a final draft. Here the meeting resembles
an autopsy and is all too likely to dwell on past failures. The theory,
supposedly, is that final-draft conferences will help students prepare
for their next paper, but the reality is that nothing is as dead, as
utterly without hope of resurrection, as a finished paper. For those
engaged in evaluation of final products, such a meeting (as has
already been argued in this book) can be better than grading papers,
but creating the give-and-take interaction of a truly effective conference is inordinately difficult.

A logistical matter for conferences that are an addition to classroom work is the scheduling problem. For high school teachers, Lois
McCallister suggests posting a list of the periods available for conferences and having students schedule times during their study hall
periods. For teachers whose schedules don't include conference periods,
McCallister suggests using seven or eight days of class time during
every six-week period for individual conferences.[38] This, in turn, raises
another problem. What do the other students do while the teacher is
holding conferences? One solution is to hold conferences at the end of

a unit so that students can begin working on the next unit with packets of materials intended to start them off.[39] When the class is planned so that students are writing continuously, there is no problem: they keep writing. If there is only time for a few conferences, Judith Kollman suggests, the first conference might be with the third paper. Her rationale is that the first paper, traditionally an in-class diagnostic, "is virtually worthless for anything but giving the student some idea of what cryptograms his instructor uses and what kinds of grades he or she dishes out; the second allows the student to pitch into his first well-considered groping toward a semi-literate, half-organized, non-development effort; by the third paper . . . he is beginning to become aware of the realities and, I trust, becoming slightly frustrated. . . . The time is ripe for the first conference."[40]

The length of a conference, depending on the format, can vary from a brief exchange of a few sentences as the teacher strolls around the room to arranged conferences which last longer. Even with scheduled conferences, Lester Fisher and Donald Murray recommend no more than fifteen minutes, at least once a week. Lest that sound like a major drain on one's time, Fisher and Murray offer some figures which should allay any apprehensions that conferences become an all-consuming way of life. As Fisher and Murray calculate their time, with fifteen-minute conferences spread over a three-day period, they can handle thirty students in seven and a half hours a week, plus one hour to scan papers in advance.[41]

Yet another solution to the time problem—and to what some see as the physical strain involved—is described by Dean Memering as simple and workable: the group conference. As used by Memering, these are editorial sessions on work in progress that focus on suggesting ways to improve drafts, eliciting ideas and information from the authors, discussing writing concepts, planning projects, and so on. These small-group sessions become seminars in writing and also steering committees for the classroom. The outcomes noted by Memering are a relaxation of defensiveness, greater rapport with each student, and a sense of participatory unity in the class as a whole. Having tried out a paper in a small-group conference, the writer is less likely to find a host of corrections on the finished paper. In addition to these major advantages, the time saving is also significant. As Memering notes, if the teacher meets with a group of six or seven students for half an hour, he or she can see a class of twenty-five in two hours.[42]

This time problem exists only for conferences tied to classroom instruction. In the writing lab, the teacher or tutor can revel in the fact that part of what labs have to offer is time, in whatever quantities the student needs. The only problems here are the waiting line of other students and the student's attention span. A perceptive tutor can tell almost immediately when a student's concentration is waning or has been diverted. Sometimes a momentary lull and some chit-chat to relieve the strain or to offer a "breather" is all that is needed before work can be resumed; sometimes momentum can be regained by a move on to some other (and perhaps fresher) topic of discussion; and sometimes the tutor simply has to recognize that some students can't sustain their interest beyond, at best, twenty minutes or half an hour.

In whatever format a teacher chooses to work there are techniques to draw on and problems that are likely to be encountered, and these are the next subjects to consider.

Notes

1. Jerome Bruner, *Toward a Theory of Instruction* (Cambridge, Mass.: Belknap Press, 1967), 53.

2. Archibald MacLeish, "On the Teaching of Writing," *Harper's Magazine,* October 1959, 160.

3. Donald Murray, "The Listening Eye: Reflections on the Writing Conference," *College English* 41 (1979): 16.

4. Donald Graves, *Writing: Teachers and Children at Work* (Portsmouth, N.H.: Heinemann, 1983), 127.

5. Lester A. Fisher and Donald Murray, "Perhaps the Professor Should Cut Class," *College English* 35 (1973): 172.

6. Quoted in Jan Turbill, *No Better Way to Teach Writing* (Rosebery, N.S.W., Australia: Primary English Teaching Association, 1982), 38.

7. Quoted in Turbill, 36–37.

8. Thomas A. Carnicelli, "The Writing Conference: A One-to-One Conversation," in *Eight Approaches to Teaching Composition,* ed. Timothy Donovan and Ben McClelland (Urbana, Ill.: National Council of Teachers of English, 1980), 111.

9. Thomas J. Reigstad and Donald A. McAndrew, *Training Tutors for Writing Conferences* (Urbana, Ill.: ERIC Clearinghouse on Reading and Communication Skills and National Council of Teachers of English, 1984), 11.

10. Stephen North, "The Idea of a Writing Center," *College English* 46 (1984): 438.

11. Judith Kollman, "How to Teach Composition on an Individual Basis— and Survive," *Journal of English Teaching Techniques* 8 (Summer 1975): 15.

12. See Muriel Harris, "Contradictory Perceptions of Rules for Writing," *College Composition and Communication* 30 (1979): 218–20; and Mike Rose, "Rigid Rules, Inflexible Plans, and the Stifling of Language: A Cognitivist Analysis of Writer's Block," *College Composition and Communication* 31 (1980): 389–401.

13. See Muriel Harris, "The Roles a Tutor Plays," *English Journal* 69 (1980): 62–65.

14. David Taylor, "A Counseling Approach to Writing Conferences" (Paper delivered at the Writing Centers Association East Central Conference, Erie, Pa., 4 May 1985), 14.

15. Murray, 17.

16. Dan Kirby and Tom Liner, *Inside Out: Developmental Strategies for Teaching Writing* (Montclair, N.J.: Boynton/Cook, 1981), 110.

17. Taylor, 2.

18. Suzanne E. Jacobs and Adela B. Karliner, "Helping Writers to Think: The Effects of Speech Roles in Individual Conferences on the Quality of Thought in Student Writing," *College English* 38 (1977): 489–505.

19. Fisher and Murray, 170.

20. Kollman, 15.

21. See Anita Brostoff, "The Writing Conference: Foundations," in *Tutoring Writing: A Sourcebook for Writing Labs,* ed. Muriel Harris (Glenview, Ill.: Scott, Foresman, 1982), 21–26; Muriel Harris, "Individualized Diagnosis: Searching for Causes, Not Symptoms of Writing Deficiencies," *College English* 40 (1978): 64–69; Stephen North, "Writing Center Diagnosis: The Composing Profile," in *Tutoring Writing: A Sourcebook for Writing Labs,* ed. Muriel Harris (Glenview, Ill.: Scott, Foresman, 1982), 42–52; and David Taylor, "Beyond Howdy Doody," *Writing Lab Newsletter,* forthcoming.

22. Joyce S. Steward and Mary K. Croft, *The Writing Laboratory* (Glenview, Ill.: Scott, Foresman, 1982), 48.

23. Sarah W. Freedman, "Evaluation in the Writing Conference: An Interactive Process," in *Selected Papers from the 1981 Texas Writing Research Conference,* ed. Maxine Hairston and Cynthia Selfe (Austin, Tex.: Univ. of Texas at Austin Press, 1981), 65–66.

24. Nancy Sommers, "Responding to Student Writing," *College Composition and Communication* 33 (1982): 154.

25. Winifred H. Harris, "Teacher Response to Student Writing: A Study of the Response Patterns of High School English Teachers to Determine the Bases for Teacher Judgment of Student Writing," *Research in the Teaching of English* 11 (1977): 175–85.

26. Barbara Fassler, "The Red Pen Revisited: Teaching Composition through Student Conferences," *College Composition and Communication* 40 (1978): 186–90.

27. Michael Blenski, Jr., "The Conference Evaluation: A Renewal," in *They Really Taught Us How to Write,* ed. Patricia Geuder, Linda Harvey, Dennis Loyd, and Jack Wages (Urbana, Ill.: National Council of Teachers of English, 1974), 136–40.

28. Donald Murray, "Teaching the Other Self," *College Composition and Communication* 33 (1982): 140–47.

29. Taylor, "A Counseling Approach," 3–7.

30. Rosemary Arbur, "The Student-Teacher Conference," *College Composition and Communication* 28 (1977): 338–42.

31. Allan Collins, Eleanor H. Warnock, and Joseph J. Passafiuma, "Analysis and Synthesis of Tutorial Dialogues," in *The Psychology of Learning and Motivation,* ed. Gordon H. Bowes (New York: Academic Press, 1975), 9:49–87.

32. Charles Cooper, "Teaching Writing by Conferencing," in *Survival through Language: The Basics and Beyond,* ed. Rita Bean, Allen Berger, and Anthony Petrosky (Pittsburgh: School of Education, Pittsburgh Univ., 1977), 16.

33. Charles Dawe and Edward Dornan, instructor's manual for *One-to-One: Resources for Conference-Centered Writing,* 2d ed. (Boston: Little, Brown, 1984).

34. Nina Luban, Ann Matsuhashi, and Tom Reigstad, "One-to-One to Write: Establishing an Individual-Conference Writing Place," *English Journal* 67 (Nov. 1978): 30–35.

35. Donald Murray, *A Writer Teaches Writing: A Practical Method of Teaching Composition* (Boston: Houghton Mifflin, 1968).

36. Graves, 98.

37. Carnicelli, 102–3.

38. Lois McCallister, "Tell Me What You Had in Mind," *English Journal* 59 (1970): 231.

39. See Blenski.

40. Kollman, 14.

41. Fisher and Murray, 172.

42. W. Dean Memering, "Talking to Students: Group Conferences," *College Composition and Communication* 24 (1973): 306–7.

3 Conference Activities

Writing conferences have goals but not predetermined directions. Like any other conversation, conference talk can follow one path for a time and then curve down another as we interact with writers. What happens during that talk? We listen, we ask questions, we observe, we demonstrate strategies, and we respond with necessary information or answers to questions. All of this, of course, goes on in the classroom, but in the conference the one-to-one situation permits a very different kind of interaction because the teacher does not (and should not) totally control the agenda. With student interaction comes the kind of unpredictability that makes lesson plans or syllabi inappropriate—and useless.

Student input in topics for discussion is also, according to Sarah W. Freedman and Anne Marie Katz, close observers of conference talk, "what makes conferences an optimal setting for learning to write."[1] As they explain, the structure of conference conversation is a cross between classroom discourse, with its preset rules for who speaks when and for how long, and natural conversation, in which speakers agree on the spot as to who speaks when. The conference, as Freedman and Melanie Sperling elaborate, is also a dialogue in which each person exercises some topical control over the flow of discourse, raising issues, shifting topics, and encouraging or discouraging elaboration.[2] In this dialogue teacher talk includes several general activities: listening, questioning, observing, showing, and telling. Because these activities are essential to the conference in different ways, let us consider each more closely.

Conversational Activities

Listening

Standing in front of their classes, teachers necessarily exert some measure of control. Even when they encourage the most freewheeling discussion, it is not conducted in a setting of total anarchy, because of the general understanding that, finally, the teacher is in charge. We

all know the rules, even if some students are reluctant to abide by
them. And for teachers, peer tutors, and students, the mutual acceptance of those rules presents problems in the conference. After years of
playing by classroom conventions, students know quite well who's in
charge. How, then, can we encourage them to become active participants in the conference conversation? Confronted with the student
who maintains the "OK, you're the teacher, so you're in control"
attitude, we have to demonstrate that the conference is indeed a
dialogue. A highly effective way to do this is to listen, thereby showing students that they can talk while we listen, that we'll listen closely
to what they say, and that they can set the agenda for what we listen to.

Though listening is a necessary activity in a conference, it is also
difficult. As Donald Graves reminds us, listening "is more a delib-
erate act than a natural one."[3] We have to put aside our personal
preferences and listen to topics we aren't interested in or even that we
disagree with. We also have to suppress a sense of uneasiness that too
much time is passing while students go on at greater length than is
needed to make a point, fall silent while mulling over what has just
been said, or decide what response to make. And because those of us
who choose the conference format usually also enjoy conversation, we
have to stifle the urge to contribute frequently and to leap in the
moment silence takes over. If we've asked a question, we must wait
and listen rather than rephrasing the question or offering clues to fill
the silence. Graves's recommendation (99) to wait at least fifteen
seconds after asking a question may seem trivially easy until we
realize how long fifteen seconds actually is. In the normal give-and-
take of an ongoing conversation, a fifteen-second pause leaves most of
us feeling uncomfortable or embarrassed for whoever was supposed to
respond and didn't. But allowing for such pauses in a conference is
crucial. Students need time to think, to weigh options, and, say
Freedman and Katz, "to internalize the substance and procedures
necessary for writing."[4]

In a conference we listen partly to hear answers to questions we
have raised, and partly to hear writers talking about their writing and
raising questions of their own. They may also mention problems they
are having, as well as evaluations of a piece of writing at whatever
stage it has progressed to. And they will talk about—or try out—their
topics, a useful precursor to writing and a beneficial means of practicing academic discourse. As Thom Hawkins explains, such talk offers
the student "the opportunity to use oral language in . . . intellectual
discourse." Using "such discourse helps teach students the skills and
judgment necessary to revise."[5] From Hawkins's experience, peer

tutors are particularly successful at helping their students practice using language because of the "intensely personal characteristics" of the social contract between tutor and student. Caring about the student's welfare, being a receptive audience, establishing the sense of mutual effort between friends, creating a feeling of closeness, providing the generous amounts of time needed to practice verbalizing—all foster the kind of setting in which, as Hawkins points out, language learners can take risks and gain the kind of language experience they need.

To develop the kind of listening needed, we have to become adept at learning how to involve the student, how to create a personal, nonthreatening, informal atmosphere for conversation that permits the student to participate actively. Establishing a nonjudgmental setting where there is no penalty for trying out ideas is as important as showing a genuine interest in what is being said. Being a good listener is, obviously, an art to be rigorously cultivated, so much so that it is surprising that the field of composition offers so little theory or research to guide us. However, we can dip into the literature available for therapists, counselors, social workers, and others who work primarily in one-to-one situations with clients. Borrowing from such sources, David Taylor recommends specific skills useful for establishing ourselves as good listeners in students' minds:[6]

1. *Paraphrasing:* restating the student's message in similar but fewer words. Hearing one's point restated by the other person is a powerful assurance that the message has been received.

2. *Perception Checking:* guessing the student's basic message and asking for affirmation of that guess. As illustrated in the conference excerpt below, this is helpful in getting a student to bring vague thoughts into sharper focus:

   Teacher: You have lots to say about hospitals. Let's try to bring it together. What would you say is the thesis of your essay?

   Student: About how most people are afraid of hospitals because they're afraid of what doctors might do to hurt them.

   Teacher: So, the thesis is "Fear of hospitals is caused by fear of pain."

   Student: That's the big part. But also there's just not knowing what will happen to them.

   Teacher: O.K. Is that a part of the thesis? A second reason for the fear of hospitals—anxiety or fear of the unknown. Is that part of it too?

> *Student:* Sure, you're in danger, at least so far as your health,
> and you're afraid of not getting well. It's hard when
> you don't know, waiting there. (14)

3. *Leading:* inviting verbal expression from the student along lines
   we prefer. *Indirect leading* gets students started and keeps responsibility on them for keeping the conference going. Thus, an
   indirect lead might be "Tell me more about . . ." A *direct lead*,
   on the other hand, asks students for precise information and
   might start off with "Give me a specific example of . . ."

4. *Interpreting:* By adding our understanding to what a student has
   already said, we can help the student see thoughts more clearly.
   When interpreting, we might start off with "so what you're saying here, then, is that . . ." (Donald Graves reminds us also that
   interpreting is needed because students sometimes say so much
   they lose track of where they are. Giving them back a summary
   or a main idea helps them to focus.)

This kind of listening involves hearing both what students say and
also what they don't say. As Taylor reminds us, so strong is the
tendency to impose our own structure or meaning on what someone
else says that we need to make a conscious effort to be open to the
reality of what that person is saying. Sometimes it is our own preferences that cause us to hear what we want to hear, and sometimes our
cultural or societal biases. Edward Hall, the cultural anthropologist,
records such a problem that occurred when a Japanese psychiatrist,
who had been observing his American colleagues, concluded that the
Americans were unresponsive to their patients' needs. The Japanese
psychiatrist, more attuned to certain elements because of his group-
oriented society, heard patients expressing a need to rely or depend on
others. The American psychiatrists, on the other hand, didn't hear
their patients express such needs because they were looking for individual problems such as depression.[7]

In a similar fashion, we are likely to overlook or ignore what we
are not disposed to hear from our students. Freedman records such a
problem in a writing conference in which the teacher and student,
reviewing the student's responses to a questionnaire, are talking about
the student's past writing courses. The teacher, assuming that the
student has a good sense of how to write a paper, does not really hear
the student's response. In fact, instead of probing to find out what the
student means by being "weak" in English, the teacher forges ahead,
following her own agenda:

> *Teacher:* But you /um/ feel that you learned some specific things.
> In other words, if you looked at your writing, you would

> have a sense of what kinds of things you need to do to produce a /hmm/ fairly good expository essay.
>
> *Student:* A little bit. But I'm really, I'm pretty weak in English.
>
> *Teacher:* Okay, oh what is, oh BCA, broadcasting, yeah, that's your major. How about in the creative writing class. Did you pick up any good techniques of writing in there?[8]

Yet another instance is recorded by Meg Hess Seckendorf, from a writing lab tutorial. Here, as Seckendorf explains, the student has been saying repeatedly that she cannot move beyond a paragraph until she thinks it's perfect. Despite the student's reiteration of this major problem, the following exchange takes place:

> *Teacher:* And, by the way, this is, what you're doing here, I've noticed, on your rough draft, you've got a lot of scratching out and things written in the margin. That's great.
>
> *Student:* Um, this was, when you see these crossouts, it was sort of, it was me saying to myself, "Just write and get down the ideas." But then I would go back. . . .[9]

The teacher here, who obviously values heavy revision, is attempting to reward the student, who, on the contrary, sees such revision as part of her problem.

As these excerpts indicate, we need not fear that students will refrain from telling us what their concerns are. Freedman's conclusion from her study of student-teacher conferences is that in a given conference, students usually have one or two top-level concerns about their writing which they will bring up repeatedly. Citing the results of similar studies of the discourse between psychiatrists and their patients, Freedman notes that these studies also reveal that "patients repeat over and over again their main concerns when talking to their psychiatrists."[10]

When we are listening closely to our students, what are we likely to hear? Students may explain the major problem(s) they are having with a paper, ask questions about the assigment, point out places where the paper is weakest, express a desire for some evaluative comments from the instructor, request help in figuring out what to do next, or ask for information (e.g., What goes in an introductory paragraph? How should a persuasive paper end? How is dialogue written on the page? When should the thesis statement be introduced?). It is fairly easy to hear what students are saying when they voice these kinds of concerns, but other matters aren't articulated so clearly. When these other concerns fill the student's mind, we have to listen more closely to hear what is being said "behind" the words. Listed below are but a few of the myriad possibilities that aren't likely to be said directly, but that need to be heard:

1. *Fear of inadequacy:* Some students, anxious about having to share writing which they are sure is inferior either to the instructor's own writing or to the instructor's taste in writing, will begin with apologies and excuses. This paper isn't their best effort because of lack of time, lack of understanding of the assignment, lack of enough previous experience with writing, or lack of something else which kept them from producing a better product. What such students are really saying is that they are sure the instructor will find the paper weak. English teachers, after all, read Shakespeare and Melville, and most students—except for budding writers—recognize their inability to compete with "the greats." These anxious students need reassurance that though we must all be able to write well everyone is not being measured by such elevated standards. A peer tutor is not as likely to hear the excuses of the insecure, because the tutor is not always perceived to be "one of them" (i.e., English teachers). But some students, overwhelmed by their own weaknesses, see even peer tutors as yet another audience ready to laugh at their poor papers.

2. *Inability to articulate the problem:* When Linda Flower and John Hayes explored the concept of writing as problem solving, they categorized writing as an ill-defined problem. Indeed, for some students, awash in confusion as to what writing is all about, writing is not merely an ill-defined problem, it is a totally mysterious process they are unable to fathom. Not having adequate words yet to talk about writing, they can't articulate very precisely what it is that they need or want help with. The teacher's first job in these cases is to help them find the words to give shape to their problems. "This paper isn't going right," "Something's missing," or "I don't know. It's just a mess" are typical opening statements of such students. They may need some conversation time to locate what that "something" is, or they might be asked if they can locate parts of the paper they dislike. They might also be helped along by means of some suggestions or even a list of possible alternatives for what that "something" might be, though there's an obvious danger here that students will grab at a suggestion, any suggestion, to end their free-floating anxiety.

3. *Mistaken notions of what teachers want:* Some students express concern about matters they think teachers care about; hence, they will ask how to "improve" (i.e., inflate) the vocabulary, lengthen the paper, correct the spelling, or whatever else it is that they think English teachers value. Such students may, if pressed, voice other—more serious—concerns about their writing, but uppermost on their lists, initially, are misconceived notions of "what the teacher wants."

4. *Lack of interest in writing:* Because of a history of not doing well in writing, because of writer's block, or because of any of the other reasons that cause students to dislike writing, a student might appear for a conference wanting nothing more than the easiest road to finishing the assignment. "What does this paper need?" such students will ask, when they mean, "What is the minimal thing I have to do to get this paper accepted?"

5. *Lack of familiarity with normal writing processes:* Some students, unaware of the messiness of real writing, mistake their groping for ideas in first drafts as an inability to write, or mistake the need to toss out or alter material during revision as being unable to get it "right" the first time. They will tell their listeners that they don't know how to write or that they can't organize their thoughts on paper when, in reality, they are merely going through the normal act of writing. In short, they will ask for help they really don't need because what they do need is some acquaintance with what writing entails.

Such lists can easily be extended, but drawing up an all-inclusive list is not necessary as long as we remember to listen closely. Diagnosis is a process that depends heavily on skilled listening and questioning.

Questioning

The clarifying questions just mentioned, to aid our listening abilities, are one type of query to use in conferences. Another set of questions, offered by Donald Murray, can reorient students to the "natural hierarchy of editorial concerns."[11] Such questions can range from "What's the single most important thing you have to say?" to "What questions is the reader going to ask you, and when?" to "Where do you hear the voice coming through strongest?" Such questions are effective because they direct the student's attention in early drafts away from the minor distractions of sentence-level editing to the major concerns of a writer. They are also effective because they are phrased in a way that invites broadly inclusive responses. Such questions, classified as "open," are the ones most likely to initiate real inquiry.

In contrast to "open" questions, Thomas J. Reigstad and David A. McAndrew classify other, less effective questions as follows:

1. *Rhetorical:* those which call for no real response from the student, for example: Shouldn't your introduction do more to interest the reader?

2. *Closed:* those which invite a yes or no or some short response from the student, for example: Is this example drawn from your own experience or from something you read?

3. *Probe and Prompt:* those which ask the student for more detail but which direct the respondent to the concerns of the person asking the question, for example: What did the house you are describing look like? How big is it? Was it made of wood, brick, or stone? Should those descriptive words be in that sentence?

4. *Leading:* those that answer themselves or lead the student to parrot information already known to the teacher, for example: What is a topic sentence? Why does your paragraph need one?[12]

It is easy to see how such questions can quash students' attempts at real conversation and make them feel that they are being tested rather than helped.

By contrast, open questions, which have the virtue of inviting fuller, more useful responses, are also the ones to use when we engage in real inquiry with students, searching for answers not yet apparent. When a student is mulling over a topic, considering ways to narrow it, seeking details to develop ideas, or weighing alternatives, we must ask the kinds of questions that indicate that there is an active search going on. If not, students assume that we are merely asking leading questions, questions we know the answers to. (This distinction is also phrased in terms of "real" questions, those we don't know the answers to, versus "exam" questions, those we are asking only to test students' knowledge.) When a student in a writing conference mistakenly thinks the teacher has the answers, all real thought ceases while the student begins searching or guessing for answers the teacher will accept. A distinct advantage peer tutors have is that students are more willing to believe that peer tutors may not know the answer themselves and are not there to quiz them.

When questioning young children in conferences, Jan Turbill advocates questions that are as specific as possible:[13]

"What words do you think you've used best?"

"Can you think of a different way to say this?"

"The words on the page don't tell me that. How could you write it to let the reader know?"

"How did you end your last piece? Is this different?"

"What part do you like best? . . . Why?"

What can questions accomplish? As already indicated, they can clarify for us and for students what problems the students are having, and they can move students away from minor editing by suggesting a more appropriate agenda of writing concerns. And they can also indicate that a real search or discovery is going on. Donald Graves adds the following to this list of what questions can do:

1. Open a conference: How is it going? What are you writing about? Where are you now in your draft?

2. Follow (or reflect) a writer's information:

    Mrs. Bagley: How is it going, Colin?

    Colin: Not so hot. I can't seem to get started.

    Mrs. Bagley: You can't get started?

    Colin: No, I always jam up after I get two lines down. I'm writing about this pet turtle I had that got lost in our car. . . .

    Mrs. Bagley: You lost the turtle in your car?

3. Deal with process: What do you think you'll do next? How will you develop/organize/revise? If you were to put new information there, how would you do it?

4. Reveal the writer's development: How did you go about writing this? How did you go about choosing your subject? What do you think of this piece of writing?

5. Deal with basic structures: What is this paper about? Is there anything else you might do with this piece?

6. Cause a temporary loss of control, to challenge a confident student to think through a problem outside the conference: What does your ending have to do with your beginning? Are you ready to handle a problem like this?[14]

Well-phrased questions are indeed a valuable teaching tool, but they are not—like some long-awaited wonder drug—an all-purpose tool. They are not, for example, the proper means for offering information or strategies. And they have disadvantages. In "Re-evaluation of the Question," JoAnn Johnson builds on educational theory that views learning as something that begins at the point of dissonance or felt need within the learner.[15] Johnson concludes from this that the learner, not the teacher, should be the one asking questions. When teachers are the ones posing questions, they are choosing the area of concern, a misplaced felt need. Questions composed by students are derived instead from the students' felt need, which should result in more involvement in learning.

Johnson also views the question as an ineffective teaching tool because its structure gives it an inhibiting power. The person being questioned becomes more involved in an attempt to offer a satisfactory response than in any mental exploration of the matter under consideration. Education, Johnson comments, is the only field where the question is considered to be a stimulant for higher levels of thinking. Professionals such as pollsters and courtroom attorneys use the question to control or inhibit thinking. Johnson finds the imperative structure a more productive strategy for her tutors to use in a writing lab conference: "If a student is told to *explain* the assignment made by the teacher, *read* a section aloud, *point* to the places that are creating discomfort or *experiment* by writing an idea in different structural styles, then she will be dealing with her needs by elaborating, manipulating and developing strategies for the identification and solving of her writing problems, and that is the goal of a writing conference."[16]

Using the imperative may be a way to sidestep the problems of the question, but such a strategy still continues to place the teacher in the position of choosing the area of felt need, of directing the conference to the teacher's priorities and concerns. And those of us who continue to value the use of questions should be encouraged by a six-year study cited by Johnson showing that teachers got better responses from students by lengthening the waiting time for students' answers. With increased wait-time the length of students' responses increased, and there were also notable increases in students' confidence, in unsolicited but appropriate responses, in student questions, and in speculative responses. A decrease in failure to respond was also noticed. The results of such a study indicate that it is well worth it, when asking questions, to wait for the answers.

Observing

In the midst of a conversation in which a teacher is both listener and questioner, the teacher also needs to lean back and observe what is going on, to observe students in order to assess their progress and problems. Assessing progress can be a matter of comparing students' present questions and comments to those in previous conferences to see if they can more easily verbalize their concerns, if they are more adept at locating trouble spots in their papers, if they have more options to explore, and if they are more aware of their readers' needs. After working with a student on several papers needing more context or explanation, a teacher can rejoice when the student casually says, "In this part here, I think I probably need to say more so you won't be confused." In this kind of observation we are placing students' present actions and words in a perspective that allows us to note their growth and progress over a semester or through a series of conferences. Instead of relying on written products, then, we should also assess the student's progress as a writer. When writing lab tutors note such growth, they can provide valuable assistance by communicating what they see to the classroom teacher.

Another kind of observing is concerned with diagnosis, a topic discussed more fully in the next chapter. Diagnosis involves watching for symptoms or causes of writing problems beyond those evident in written products. A major benefit of the conference is that it permits the teacher to look beyond the product to the person writing the paper. Thus, some papers will exhibit problems which students themselves can correct, if coaxed to do so. In the following brief excerpt, the student doesn't know the grammatical rule involved, but is able nevertheless to spot a problem and to offer a solution for a revised version:

Teacher: There's a problem . . . this sentence. Would you please read it aloud and see if you think everything sounds all right to your ear?

Student: "Calculus and modern history are two courses I signed up for, and they are of different hardness."

Teacher: How does that sound to you?

Student: Not so good . . . ahhh . . . I'm not sure what you call it. Can you say "different hardness"? I wasn't sure when I wrote it if . . .

Teacher: Well, try explaining that in another way that sounds better to you.

Student: I signed up for calculus, which is a hard course, and I also decided to take modern history, which is also hard, but in a different way.

At other times, however, papers have problems which students can't identify and therefore can't correct. Asked if anything didn't sound right or if she could spot any problem in the sentence "She was so overdressed with hair always encased in hair spray," another student was unable to offer any suggestions for what might be trouble spots in that sentence. Similarly, students who use phrases like "bored of" something or "real well" probably also use such constructions in their speech and need to be told that these phrases are not correct usage. During the puzzled silence that usually follows in the wake of a correction, we can help by inserting a quick lesson on usage—a few sentences explaining that not everything we say or hear is correct, that textbooks list some of the more common confusions, and that we will also try to help the writer identify other usage errors.

When listening to students' speech and asking students to self-correct, we can decide which students need proofreading strategies to catch their own errors and which students need information or some further study of whatever rules they are unable to apply. We also need to observe students as they write, to see whether they notice errors on the page, whether they stop too often to edit what they have written (thereby interfering with their ability to compose), whether they reread whole sentences as they revise, or whether they revise locally, leaving mismatched parts of sentences on the page, and so on. Whatever it is we are looking for, direct observation is an effective tool available to us during conferences.

In addition, we can also use the conference to observe whether students have necessary writing strategies at their disposal or are in need of some assistance. In a conference where a paper is being planned, for example, we can see whether the student needs more effective invention strategies and, if so, suggest better ones. Or, when students appear—as they occasionally do in the writing lab where I teach—with a shuffle of notecards, random bits of paper, and maybe a photocopy of a few pages from some book, we need to talk about ways to organize material before drafting begins. Watching students revise, even just a sentence or two, we can also easily spot those students who have no handy way of inserting new material on an overcrowded page. Intervening with some suggestions here can be of great help, the kind of assistance we are not likely to offer in a classroom. Similarly, when we observe students using ineffective proofreading strategies, we can share techniques that work for us.

Showing

Having carefully observed students in order to sense their needs, we can intervene in a number of ways, and one way to do so, as suggested above, is to *show* a student how to do something. The conference is a natural and easy environment for such demonstrations, especially when the demonstration includes an opportunity for the student to practice what is being shown. Demonstrating how to brainstorm, for example, can usefully be done in a conference because descriptions of what is supposed to happen during brainstorming are often too vague or mysterious for students. Inviting a student to join us in a brain-storming session can be a far more productive first step than letting the student try it alone or with another student equally unsure of the process. Showing students what it's like to use various invention questions is another useful conference activity, as is making outlines or tree diagrams, taking notes, or using one or another proofreading strategy. Rather than talking about what these techniques are, it's easier—and clearer—to illustrate what we mean by actually taking the student through them. Anyone who has learned a process in the com-pany of an expert (from playing a violin to flipping pancakes) can vouch for the benefits of having someone "go through the motions" with us.

When showing students what to do, we can accompany them, have them join in, or demonstrate for them. Demonstrating, or "model-ing," is a recognized teaching technique with an extensive body of research (summarized in "Modeling")[17] to support its effectiveness. Teachers who may be hesitant about their ability to perform success-fully in the spotlight while students watch can be comforted by studies showing that the most skilled models (usually termed "mastery models") are not the most effective teachers. On the contrary, when students watch models who are not very good at what they are doing but who become more confident as they proceed, they seem to gain more than they would by watching models who begin and end at the same high level of competence.

When modeling some aspect of writing, we can follow several guidelines to ensure better learning:

1. The model should explain what it is that he or she is demon-strating.

2. As the model proceeds through the process, he or she should comment on or call attention to the important features of what he or she is doing.

3. During or after the modeling session, he or she can ask the student to summarize what was observed.

4. The model can ask the student to practice what he or she just observed, and as the student goes through the process offer the student feedback on what he or she is doing.

Modeling can also be a classroom activity, of course, but it is par-ticularly effective in the one-to-one setting of the conference because students can ask questions and get instant feedback when they try the process. Moreover, in the relaxed, personal atmosphere of a conference, both the model and the student are relieved of the strain of performing in front of an audience. My own experience with modeling (described in "Modeling") proved to me both what an effective tool it is for conference teaching and how pleasant it can be for teacher and student to "play" together. In an attempt to help one severely blocked writer, I resorted to demonstrating free-writing as a way to show him how to overcome his preference for endless planning aloud rather than committing words to paper. As we gave each other topics and engaged in free-writing while speaking aloud the words we were writing (so that the other person could hear what was going on), we often bumbled in our haste to get words on paper. Tape recordings of these sessions indicate that a good deal of time was spent giggling at our own ineptness. This may seem like a waste of valuable time, but the result is a relaxed working relationship that greatly reduces the tension level for students, particularly those having major difficulties with writing. Clearly, too little attention has been paid to the merits of game playing and humor in the teaching of writing.

While modeling may involve lengthy (and repeated) demonstrations for major strategies, some techniques may require only brief sessions. Explaining how to proofread for misspellings or word omissions on a page, telling the student to slow down and read carefully, word by word, for example, is less helpful (and less vivid) than simply going through a few lines at an appropriate speed, with pencil in hand to point to specific words. Other techniques, such as sorting out and organizing unruly collections of ideas and notes for a paper, can be brief for some students but may require several demonstrations in order for other students to acquire a feeling for how to proceed. (Material for such demonstrations and practice is available in *Practice for a Purpose.*)[18]

But whatever it is we choose to demonstrate and to have students demonstrate back to us, showing is a valuable tool for conferences because it can bring alive for the student a writing process or strategy that has seemed shrouded in the mystery of textbook descriptions. A similar process is illustrated in one American's description of her experiences when training a group of Vietnamese to cope with the complexities of American life before arriving in the United States. Using diagrams and a lengthy verbal description, she tried to acquaint them with the process of using a coin-operated telephone. Patient repetitions seemed to produce little result, despite the people's eagerness to master the steps involved. Finally, in desperation, the teacher constructed a mock-up of an American pay phone, carried it to class, went through the steps, and achieved resounding success with a thirty-second demonstration.

Telling

While some aspects of writing can be shown, others are best explained. When working inductively, we ask questions to lead students from example to generalization, but some matters can be handled more efficiently and effectively in a deductive approach. If we want to call attention to a spelling error, explain bibliographic format, or review an assignment, it is not worth the time or effort to lead the student through questioning to the answer. Instead, telling the student the general principle is a more productive approach. And, sometimes, what we need to tell students is not a principle but some necessary information. For example, students who haven't provided enough specific details need to hear from a reader that what is offered on paper is too general. Organizational suggestions, explanations of some grammatical rule, even guidelines for what makes an effective title are also matters that can be introduced deductively by telling students some information that is needed before proceeding. Student and teacher can then work together to transfer this generalized information to the student's own writing.

The difficulty, of course, lies in knowing what is best to elicit from students inductively, what is best shown to them, and what is most effectively offered by telling them. People who lecture to large groups seem to have an easier time of it. They more often rely on telling, sometimes at great length, sometimes in an informative, memorable way, sometimes with aids such as slides, but always in the basic modes of telling and showing. In the conference, these are only two of a number of options. When teachers in conferences try to decide if telling is appropriate, they can gain a clearer perspective on this deductive approach by considering its use by counselors in therapy sessions.

Directive versus Nondirective Approaches

When counselors choose between directive and nondirective approaches in guiding therapy sessions, they do so in light of their purposes and goals. The directive approach, as described in "The Student-Centered Conference and the Writing Process," by Charles Duke, favors the didactic and prescriptive and operates on the assumption that a client has come for advice and help.[19] Therefore, the responsibility of the counselor, who presumably has more expertise in the field that does the client, is to identify the client's problems and to offer remedies. Such an approach can solve the client's difficulties, but it can also cause the client to resist any advice that is offered because he or she feels intimidated by the directness and often the bluntness of the advice. In contrast, the nondirective approach rests on the assumption that most people can help themselves if they are freed from emotional obstacles such as fear of criticism and fear of failure. The role of the counselor in a nondirective conference is to allow clients to relax and talk freely about how they might solve their own problems.

Though Duke cautions against drawing too many parallels between the writing conference and a counseling session, he recommends that we consider the use of some nondirective strategies:

1. *Focusing:* We can help the student understand what is going to happen in the conference, what is expected of each person, how long the conference will last, and, possibly, what the results will be. This can provide the student with some security.

2. *Clarifying:* We can help students understand what they have expressed in a paper and show that what they have said is appreciated.

3. *Using acceptance and approval words:* Because students too often view themselves as failures, we can offer signs of approval, even such simple affirmations as "yes" and "I see."

4. *Using reassuring phrases:* We can show students that they are not alone and that others share similar feelings and thoughts.

5. *Providing nondirective leads:* We can encourage students to talk about their writing by means of questions such as "Could this section be stated in more than one way?"

In Reigstad and McAndrew's description of the writing conference, the techniques of nondirective questioning and supportive comments can be incorporated into various stages of the conversation.[20] At the beginning of a conference, the teacher can use focusing and give nondirective leads to help the student understand what is going to happen and to let the student take the initiative in determining the direction of the conversation. Throughout the conference the teacher can use clarification, asking for additional information or restating what the student means, in order both to help the student understand what has been communicated in each draft and to show that the writing is interesting. Using acceptance words that reflect agreement, along with comprehension of what was said—without expressing value judgments—will foster a student's self-esteem. When students appear to need more than acceptance or approval, teachers can offer reassuring phrases, expressing a shared feeling or thought.

The value of such nondirective techniques, as Duke concludes (46), is that they are an effective means for reducing teacher-centered talk and avoiding the traditional overdirection of teacher-centered conferences. Such an approach also encourages students to become more responsive to new ideas about writing and provides the kind of acceptance and approval that help to build writers' confidence. In addition, students are provided with live, responsive audiences for their writing and are encouraged to accept responsibility for their writing processes.

While advocates of using nondirective techniques for the writing conference are emphatic about the benefits of such techniques, they also note their potential drawbacks, especially the considerable time required for such conversation. And for teachers who see lack of time as a major obstacle to using conferences in the teaching of writing, conversation that takes the long way home may simply be a luxury they cannot afford. The counterargument, of course, is akin to that used by people who oppose America's infatuation with fast food: quicker is not usually better.

While the arguments for directive and nondirective approaches pertain to students we normally consider "typical," we also need to remember that teaching strategies appropriate for these students are not necessarily effective for other groups such as the learning disabled. As reported by Leone Scanlon in "Learning Disabled Students at the Writing Center," the learning disabled students who use the Clark University Writing Center, which she directs, expressed anxiety, frustration, and anger in response to the standard tutoring strategies of questioning students to elicit their responses.[21] More guidance is necessary to reduce the anxiety they all too often feel in a nondirective setting. (Other suggestions for strategies to use in working with the learning disabled are described by Paula Gills, Jacqueline Lauby, Helen Mills, and David Taylor.)[22]

Uses of Language and Other Forms of Communication

Verbal Communication

Yet another dimension of the conference to consider is the teacher's various forms of communication, both in spoken and nonverbal language. As we talk or listen, question or demonstrate, elicit responses or offer guidance, we depend on the flow of conversation to carry our meaning. But other messages are being communicated in the words we choose, in our actions, in our gestures—even in what we do not do.

In our verbal communication, we obviously need to monitor the speed and level of complexity of our speech, and we need to acquire a working vocabulary of terms students can understand. In each conference, this level must be adjusted to the particular student, especially if we think we need to refer to specialized terms of our field or some grammatical jargon. Can we talk to one student about "independent clauses"? Does another student understand "coherence," or should we either explain the term or find a substitute? We ought to consider whether some students would profit from knowing a few basic terms so that they too can talk about their writing. And we should acquire a repertoire of words to convey reactions which are neither harsh judgments nor implied attacks on the student as a person. Journal articles drip with disgust over the use of such terms as "awkward" and "disorganized," yet these denunciations continue to litter the margins of student papers and devastate the writers. "Teacher talk" is what Jay Jacoby calls jargon-laden and judgmental comments, a form of communication he helps the tutors in his writing center to avoid.[23]

An added complication is that we need to monitor not only what we say to students generally, but also what we say to *each* student. As Sarah W. Freedman's studies of conference conversation have shown, a teacher has different relationships with different students in the same class. The result, as described in Freedman and Sperling's "Teacher-Student Interaction in the Writing Conference" (40-41), is different instruction. For high- and low-achieving students, for example, the teacher studied focused on different types of topics for each. She also gave more expository explanations and more praise to the higher-achieving students, who seemed to elicit it by their comments.

Because praise and positive reinforcement are so important, we also need to acquire a vocabulary of terms that convey to students that their writing has value and merit. Positive reinforcement, described by Hayes and Daiker as the most important tool available to enlightened composition teachers,[24] is needed to give the writer confidence to do some experimenting and courage to keep trying. But praise has other uses as well, because writers need to know what is working well in a paper. If they don't recognize an effective part of a paper, they may delete it from the next draft.

Though praise is important—even necessary—for the development of writers, compliments may not always convey the intended message, especially with foreign students. In a study of compliments as perceived by non-native students, Nessa Wolfson concluded that what is considered a compliment may differ greatly from one society to another. For example, one international student reported to Wolfson that the compliment which says to a person that he or she looks unusually good (for example: "Your hair looks great! I almost didn't recognize you!") can imply to someone not familiar with the convention that the reverse is usually the case. Wolfson also reports that people from cultures less open in expressions of approval are often extremely embarrassed by what they consider the excessive complimenting Americans indulge in. This is not to say that we cannot praise ESL students, only that we should monitor our praise to see that it conveys what we wish it to.

Nonverbal Communication

Because body language also conveys messages, we need to consider even the physical arrangements of a conference. The traditional teacher-at-the-desk and student-sitting-at-the-side arrangement conveys a hierarchy of control not likely to be conducive to an informal interchange of conversation, nor to promote the feeling that the teacher is a coach/counselor/editor. Much more effective is the side-by-side meeting of two people looking at a paper that is best kept in front of the student rather than the teacher. Nodding, smiling to show agreement, and offering other small but significant human gestures of friendliness and approval are additional means of conveying our messages.

Nonverbal Communication Problems between Cultures

Lest we get too caught up in worrying about nonverbal communication, Edward Hall, the anthropologist, warns us against attaching specific meaning to specific actions. His studies have demonstrated that "the meaning of a communication is always dependent upon the context."[25] But Hall's work in cross-cultural communication should also serve as a warning against imposing patterns of American cultural behavior on those of our students who do not share the dominant American culture (or, if teachers are not members of the dominant American culture, of carrying patterns of behavior from another culture into the conference). One example of difficulties that can arise in a conference between two people with different cultural orientations has to do with the distance between the two people. Americans, as Hall explains in *The Silent Language,* have a pattern which discourages touching and which avoids bodily contact.[26] Thus, Americans tend to keep their distance when speaking and may even back up when another person comes too close. In Latin American cultures, however, interaction distance is much less, and people can talk comfortably at ranges closer than Americans would be at ease with. The result can be a conversation in which a Latin American moves closer to a North American in order to be at a more comfortable distance, thereby causing the North American to back away. As a consequence of this dance of retreat, the Latin American may think the North American is being distant or cold, withdrawn, and unfriendly.

Even the matter of eye contact differs among cultures. Eye behavior in a conversation is important because it signals whether the other person is listening and whether the speaker is being understood. Yet many ambiguities in conversation arise from different uses of the eye. As Hall has observed,[27] the English signal that they have heard by blinking their eyes, while Americans typically look the other person in the eye when they want to be sure that they are getting their message across. However, Americans are apt to be made uncomfortable by the intensity with which Arabs look at each other. Blacks, on the other hand, are less prone to using eye contact and have been misinterpreted by American whites as being uninterested and unmotivated because of lack of eye contact in job interviews.[28] When we consider the havoc of miscommunication that can result from such differences, we can easily realize why we need to tread carefully when using our own criteria to interpret nonverbal communication by members of other cultures.

There also exists the possibility that our behavior will be misinterpreted by students from other cultures. Even the relatively minor matter of chair placement has proven to be a source of annoyance, as documented in Hall's work. In *The Hidden Dimension* (137–38), Hall describes Americans' preference for adjusting their chairs to the social situation; if need be, they will move their chairs to what they consider the appropriate distance for a conversation. Yet to the Germans Hall observed and questioned, this was upsetting, disturbing their sense of the order established in a room. For one German newspaper editor who had moved to the United States, Americans' habit of adjusting their chairs to the situation when they came to his office so irritated him that he had his visitor's chair bolted to the floor.

Obviously, we cannot foresee every possibility for miscommunication with students, especially since so little is known about cross-cultural communication and since even those differences noted by students of the field are merely general tendencies, not universals true of every person in that group. What is important is to remain sensitive to the needs and reactions of the students sitting next to us and to be wary of absolute reliance on our own interpretations of other people's behavior.

Conference Problems

In addition to monitoring words and gestures, we also have to be prepared to cope with a variety of problems that can arise in a conference setting. Even experienced teachers find that the conference provides a fertile environment for a variety of difficulties to breed. The time problem is one such difficulty. Because a conference is usually not concluded by a ringing bell, it can easily run overtime when we forget to pace ourselves by means of an internal alarm clock which gauges not only the time allotted but also the length of the waiting line of other students. If we notice that we are prone to running overtime in general, we need to reassess our notion that we are holding fifteen-minute or half-hour sessions and schedule students accordingly. Keeping students stacked up like a doctor's waiting room does no more for their dispositions that it does for ours when we are caught up in such delays. Calling an end to a session with a student not yet ready to leave can also cause time problems. Acknowledging that strict schedules are difficult in such a setting is one way to deal with the time problem; allowing spare time between conferences to use if needed is another method.

Overburdening the conference with an agenda that is too long is another problem that can arise. Teachers used to marking all noticeable errors, weaknesses, and strengths in a paper may feel the need to do so in a verbal evaluation, especially with basic writers or international students who are more prone to having numerous surface errors in their writing. A page with multitudinous grammatical mistakes seems to invite a comment or explanation for each error, but this burdens the conference with too many matters for discussion, even if some are very brief. The conference loses focus, goes on too long, and is in grave danger of being totally teacher-dominated. Instead, it is important for us to remember that it is far more effective to concentrate on a thorough discussion of one or two topics than to range far and wide, touching briefly on much more than the student is likely to remember ten minutes after the conference is over.

Despite our best intentions, conferences can also go awry because of some difficulty on the student's part. A session with a passive, unresponsive, or indifferent student may never become the kind of instructional interchange that we hope for because we find ourselves instead expending too much effort in coping with the student's reserve. Hostile students are usually so consumed by the cause of their anger that they cannot divert their attention until they vent some steam. With overly talkative students who keep offering extraneous talk or endless personal anecdotes, we may find it difficult to keep switching the conversation back to writing concerns. Other students are so eager to please that they respond with "I see . . . OK . . . I understand" long before they really do. And then there are manipulative students interested in getting us to do all the work. They wait for the teacher to do the thinking necessary to answer the question hanging in the air, and they are likely to keep prodding the teacher to show them not only what's wrong in the paper but also how to correct it. Though students—and teachers—in a conference are prone to all the usual human failings, such problems do divert our attention away from our larger purposes, and the challenge is to keep our goals in mind. Trading war stories (as tutors in tutor-training courses can do) is an excellent way of keeping our perspective, maintaining our sense of humor, and acquiring strategies for dealing with these problems.

For tutors who work with their peers, there are some added problems unique to the situation. Peer tutors, sensitive to the need to establish their authority as "teachers," are in danger of forgetting their great strength, that they are obviously helpers or coaches, not evaluators. Peer tutors I've observed focus too much initially on their fear of making a mistake or not knowing the right answer to tell the student. Peer tutors can only put aside these fears when they begin to realize that most students prefer working with a friendly helper rather than facing yet another authority figure who knows all the answers. Another source of comfort for peer tutors is knowing that help is available nearby from a fellow peer tutor or teacher. An atmosphere in which peer tutors are free to admit that they are not infallible and that they too are seeking answers is equally encouraging to students who then see that learning to write well is a quest in which we are all involved. Sharing in the search also reminds students that they too are expected to contribute and that they need not worry that they don't know the answers as they seek them. Reminding everyone of the old maxim "Only the truly stupid are too dumb to ask" helps considerably.

Despite the lengthy list of problems discussed above, those new to the conference approach will undoubtedly find themselves in situations not even hinted at here—and experienced teachers will have their own lists to contribute. But the conference offers no more quagmires to the unwary than any other teaching situation. It merely has its own unique situations. The conference is nevertheless a setting with a more congenial atmosphere in which to deal with problems, for in the friendly informality of two people working together, situations can be dealt with in a more open, comfortable way.

Notes

1. Sarah W. Freedman and Anne Marie Katz, "Pedagogical Interaction during the Composing Process: The Writing Conference," in *Writing in Real Time: Modeling Production Processes,* ed. Ann Matsuhashi (Norwood, N.J.: Ablex, forthcoming).

2. Sarah W. Freedman and Melanie Sperling, "Written Language Acquisition: The Role of Response and the Writing Conference," in *The Acquisition of Written Language: Response and Revision,* ed. Sarah W. Freedman (Norwood, N.J.: Ablex, 1985).

3. Donald Graves, *Writing: Teachers and Children at Work* (Portsmouth, N.H.: Heinemann, 1983), 100.

4. Freedman and Katz, "Pedagogical Interaction."

5. Thom Hawkins, "Intimacy and Audience: The Relation between Revision and the Social Dimension of Peer Tutoring," *College English* 42 (1980): 64–68.

6. David Taylor, "A Counseling Approach to Writing Conferences" (Paper delivered at the Writing Centers Association East Central Conference, Erie, Pa., 4 May 1985), 13–16.

7. Quoted in Gary Blonston, "The Translator," *Science 85* 6, no. 6 (1985), 83.

8. Sarah W. Freedman, *Teaching and Learning in the Writing Conference* (Urbana, Ill.: ERIC Clearinghouse on Reading and Communication Skills, 1980), ED 185 599, 13.

9. Meg Hess Seckendorf, "The Dynamics of a Student-Tutor Conference: A Case Study" (Paper delivered at the Conference on College Composition and Communication, Minneapolis, 22 March 1985), 5.

10. Freedman, *Teaching and Learning,* 4.

11. Donald Murray, "Teaching the Other Self," *College Composition and Communication* 33 (1982): 145.

12. Thomas J. Reigstad and Donald A. McAndrew, *Training Tutors for Writing Conferences* (Urbana, Ill.: ERIC Clearinghouse on Reading and Communication Skills and National Council of Teachers of English, 1984), 3.

13. Jan Turbill, *No Better Way to Teach Writing* (Rosebery, N.S.W., Australia: Primary English Teaching Association, 1982), 35.

14. Graves, 107–17.

15. JoAnn B. Johnson, "Re-evaluation of the Question as a Teaching Tool," *Writing Lab Newsletter* 10, no. 4 (1985): 1–4.

16. Johnson, 4.

17. Muriel Harris, "Modeling: A Process Method of Teaching," *College English* 45 (1983): 74–84.

18. Muriel Harris, *Practice for a Purpose* (Boston: Houghton Mifflin, 1984).

19. Charles R. Duke, "The Student-Centered Conference and the Writing Process," *English Journal* 64 (1975): 44–47.

20. Reigstad and McAndrew, 5.

21. Leone Scanlon, "Learning Disabled Students at the Writing Center," *Writing Lab Newsletter* 9, no. 5 (1985): 9–11.

22. Paula Gills, "A Reader Responds," *Writing Lab Newsletter* 9, no. 8 (1985): 6–8; Jacqueline Lauby, "Understanding the Dyslexic Writer," *Writing Lab Newsletter* 9, no. 5 (1985): 7–9; Helen Mills, "Diagnosing Writing Problems and Identifying Learning Disabilities in the Writing Lab," in *Tutoring Writing: A Sourcebook for Writing Labs*, ed. Muriel Harris (Glenview, Ill.: Scott, Foresman, 1982), 74–83; and David Taylor, "Identifying and Helping the Dyslexic Writer," *Journal of Developmental Education* 9, no. 2 (1985): 8–11.

23. Jay Jacoby, "Shall We Talk to Them in 'English'? The Contributions of Sociolinguistics to Training Writing Center Personnel," in *Proceedings of the Writing Centers Association Fifth Annual Conference,* ed. Muriel Harris and Tracey Baker (West Lafayette, Ind.: Dept. of English, Purdue University, 1983), 108–32.

24. Mary F. Hayes and Donald Daiker, "Using Protocol Analysis in Evaluating Responses to Student Writing," *Freshman English News* 13, no. 2 (1984): 4.

25. Edward T. Hall, *Beyond Culture* (Garden City, N.Y.: Doubleday, Anchor Press, 1977), 82.

26. Edward T. Hall, *The Silent Language,* (New York: Doubleday, 1959), 191, 205, 209.

27. Edward T. Hall, *The Hidden Dimension,* (Garden City, N.Y.: Doubleday, Anchor Press, 1969), 143.

28. Blonston, 81.

4 Diagnosis for Teaching One-to-One

It has been said that grading a paper at home without the writer nearby is like judging a golfer's talents and weaknesses by looking at his scorecard back at the clubhouse. Like many pungent metaphors, this too is an overstatement, though it does highlight the tendency to rely on the product or result for an analysis of the process that produced it. In the conference, however, we are able to look beyond products to the writers who produced them in order to determine the help needed. In conferences, in fact, products aren't even necessary to initiate the instruction, because we can begin working with the writer before words ever appear on paper and continue working as drafts develop. At every stage of interaction with writers we listen and ask about what is being written (or planned) in order to encourage the writer, to offer feedback as readers, and to diagnose writing skills problems in order to determine what, if any, our instructional help should be. William Irmscher asks us to consider what the basis of that help will be when he asks: "Does instruction in writing consist of telling students what we know about the process of writing or using what we know to diagnose their difficulties and helping them solve their problems?"[1] Diagnosis is the necessary basis for—and precursor of—instruction.

Diagnosis is a highly complex act because, like writing, it is a set of intertwining processes that can and do occur simultaneously. We must consider what the student is doing, what the writing reveals, what lenses we are looking through, and what is involved in the skills needed. Consider, for example, the following sentence:

> Then I ate all three sandwiches very slowly as I stared at my mom
> while I ate them she knew I wanted her to notice me.

To identify this as a run-on sentence is merely to label an error, but such a label is not a diagnosis because it doesn't consider the particular writer (what she knows, how she writes, and how she learns), the writing (what the context of the error is), the teacher (what our goals for that student are), or the error (what is involved in being able to understand the appropriate grammatical rule).

In addition to considering all these aspects, we also have to be aware that, like writing, diagnosis is a process that unfolds, that requires backtracking as well as forward motion. That is, we may generate some ideas about what to help the student with, only to find as we progress, because of new information, that our suppositions were wrong, incomplete, or shortsighted. One problem may be masking another, deeper one that needs to be dealt with, or we may have thought the cause of a problem to be one thing when it becomes apparent later that another cause is more likely. Or a better alternative suddenly suggests itself. All this complexity, however, should not stifle our diagnostic efforts because, as with the process of writing, no one waits until every subprocess is mastered before plunging in. And, as with writing, the best way to get better at it is by doing it.

The Teacher

Evaluation Criteria

One aspect of diagnosis is to take a close look at ourselves and what we teach. Do we see our function as editing the paper or helping the writer develop? Do we react to certain writing problems more readily than to others? Is there a pattern to these reactions? For example, are we prone to reacting more strongly to grammatical errors because we have a low tolerance for surface error on a page, because grammatical error is easier to identify, or because we see our role as teachers of correctness? Does concern with sentence-level correctness block our ability to look beyond the errors to the ideas expressed? Or do we ignore grammatical errors, hoping they will disappear somehow because we don't know how to help students overcome them, because we find it tedious to teach grammatical rules, or because mechanical correctness is not a high priority in our evaluation of writing? Do we value style more than organization? Are we prone to rewarding the five-paragraph essay or recoiling from it?

Whatever criteria we use, we must be conscious of those criteria and how they influence and color what we see on paper and hear from the student. We also have to consider all the evaluation criteria our students have absorbed from previous teachers of writing and the degree to which those criteria may differ from ours. And, finally, as studies reported by John Daly indicate, we should acknowledge that there is a tendency among teachers to expect better writing from students who are less apprehensive about writing than from students who are more apprehensive.[2]

Teaching Methods and Styles

We also need to consider *how* we teach, because that will influence how we gather information and what we do with the results of our diagnosis. Since we all have preferred modes of learning, it follows that we will present information and suggestions in accord with the ways that we ourselves learn or gather and process information. Matching, or mismatching, our preferences with those of our students is a major concern. If, for example, we tend to conceptualize visually, will our diagrams and drawings be a good way to help all students learn, or should we attempt to consider their preferences as well? Though we deal well with discrete units of information, does the student perhaps need more context? When learning styles are mismatched, the unfortunate result, as experimental evidence has shown, is that student understanding and retention drop markedly.[3]

Composing Styles

And then there are questions of our own composing processes. If we tend to do our planning in our heads, are we offering inappropriate advice to the student who prefers to write down every option on paper before crossing some out? If we use outlines in our own composing, do we therefore see a disorganized draft of a student paper as an indication of lack of direction—even if the student habitually needs discovery draft after discovery draft to begin defining the point of the paper? Or, conversely, do we diagnose an overconcern with editing skills in early drafts if we prefer to delay such practices until later? Do we insist on extensive prior planning and exploration with writers who are more comfortable with exploring as they proceed through free-writing drafts? If we remember some childhood embarrassment about our spelling mistakes, do we unconsciously assume the bad spellers we meet now feel similar embarrassment? Other possible interferences can be listed indefinitely. The point, however, is that we should not diagnose student writing problems or offer help using only ourselves as yardsticks or allowing our preferences to be imposed on our students. Of course, it will happen, especially when so little is known about individual differences in all these areas, but being cognizant of the problem may keep us from committing excesses.

The Student

Differences in Personality Types

Attempts to identify individual differences among composing styles have produced a number of approaches and taxonomies, and while these may not yet have been sufficiently verified by large-scale research, they do offer windows into the differences we note among our students, differences that can be helpful in diagnostic work. One such system, developed by George Jensen and John DiTiberio, is based on the work of Carl Jung (later refined by Isabel Meyers) on personality types.[4] This system differentiates four bipolar dimensions, each of which represents opposing psychological processes:

1. "extraversion" (to preserve Jung's spelling)-introversion (ways of focusing one's energies)
2. sensing-intuition (ways of perceiving)
3. thinking-feeling (ways of making evaluations and decisions)
4. judging-perceiving (ways of approaching tasks in the outer world)

To relate these dimensions to writing processes, Jensen and DiTiberio observed several groups of writers and concluded that writers who are extraverts tend to leap into tasks with little planning, relying instead on trial and error to complete the tasks. They think more clearly and develop more ideas while in action or conversation and need feedback and interaction. Introverts, on the other hand, anticipate and reflect beforehand, and they think best and develop more ideas when they are alone. Although they do need to plan, too much planning can cause them to block. Such distinctions suggest that we acknowledge some students' increased need for conference time to plan their writing since the interchange can be productive. Jensen and DiTiberio's description also suggests that, in addition, we need to watch for the possibility that other students are best left to work on their own, as conference conversation may not be an effective planning tool for them. We would also expect that some extraverts might need more drafts to develop effective products because their trial-and-error approach could require more rewriting and revising than that of introverts.

Sensing and intuition, the second dimension in this system, are personality types differing in that sensing types make more direct use of their perceptions. They are oriented toward concrete details, while intuitive types use impressions and their imaginations and are oriented toward ideas. In telling stories, sensing types use reality as their starting point, that is, what happened when, and so on; intuitive types, on the other hand, are likely to start with what sensing types save for last, namely, the meaning behind events. To understand concepts, sensing types need concrete examples, and they write best when given explicit, detailed instructions, preferably step-by-step procedures. When they write, sensing types may find it easier when they are given a specific framework, and they attend closely to mechanics, often seeing revising as merely correcting. Intuitive types, on the other hand, write best when given general instructions from which they can create their own goals. They can become blocked by their need for originality, and their first drafts may contain only ideas and generalities unsupported by concrete examples. For diagnostic purposes these differences lend themselves readily to understanding what each type needs to work on. For example, we would focus on helping intuitive writers bring more examples and details to their early drafts, and we would want to be sure that we use concrete examples when explaining anything to a sensing type. Sensing types may also have difficulties in doing the large-scale "re-seeing" that is needed for revision since, as Jensen and DiTiberio have noted, they have a tendency to look more for mechanical errors to fix as they move to later drafts of their papers.

The third dimension in this personality type system, thinking and feeling, describes how one makes evaluations, judgments, and decisions. Thinking types, as described by Jensen and DiTiberio, prefer to make decisions on the basis of objective criteria and excel at the process of categorizing, whereas feeling types prefer to make decisions on the basis of subjective factors such as personal values. Moreover, thinking types need clear, objective performance standards, focus on clarity of content, usually follow an outline as an organizational pattern, and may need to enliven their writing with vivid personal examples when revising. In contrast, feeling types need to relate their personal values to topics. They tend to focus on how an audience may react, worrying that the audience will be bored or find the ideas inadequate. When revising, they may need to clarify their thoughts or improve their organization. They will be less likely to follow outlines, which may be constraining for them. In the conference setting, we would expect students who fall at either end of this spectrum to voice very different goals for their papers, with thinking types interested in clarity and feeling types more concerned about their readers' reactions. Thinking types might also want clear-cut assignment guidelines for what their papers are to be and how the papers will be evaluated, while feeling types may be more likely to handle open-ended assignments comfortably.

Finally, the fourth dimension is judging-perceiving. Judging types tend to be decisive, to limit their topics quickly, and to set manageable goals. Before writing they devote time to what Linda Flower and John Hayes call process goals (how to get things done).[5] They make stylistic and organizational decisions quickly, so when they revise they need to consider the implications of their data or ideas and to expand their writing to clarify or qualify bluntly worded statements. They are also in danger of adhering to plans too rigidly. Unlike judging types, perceiving types tend not to limit their topics. Their first drafts are often long and thorough, but too inclusive. They tend to feel that they must write everything that could be written on a subject. Jensen and DiTiberio's distinctions suggest that revision will be a matter of seeing what to expand upon, for judging types, and what to chop out, for perceiving types.

Students will not, of course, fit themselves neatly at one end or the other of any of these spectra, but we can see from the range of preferences described above that we should expect great diversity in our students. Rather than feeling overwhelmed by the welter of differences we see, however, we can take comfort in knowing that the conference setting will allow us to offer more appropriate instruction than is available in the large-group setting of the classroom. Part of that instruction will be to help students understand how their preferences guide their composing. We can also help students work in ways unfamiliar to them, for, as Jensen and DiTiberio have observed, writers function best when their early drafts draw upon their preferred processes and later drafts on unpreferred modes to round out the writing. For example, intuitive types may need help in adding sensory detail, while feeling types may need more work on organization. We can also use an awareness of these personality dimensions to recognize that students' difficulties may be due to assignments which are structured in ways that will cause them problems, as when sensing types flounder when given the kind of general writing assignments that intuitive types can handle more easily. And these distinctions also help to structure the ways in which we help different students learn, working from example to concept for sensing types and from concept to example for intuitive types.

Differences in Cognitive Styles

Another system for differentiating among writers is that of distinguishing various cognitive styles, that is, how people process information. Mike Rose's case study data for his work on writing blocks suggest to him at least three composing styles based on differences in cognitive styles:

1. The ruminative style (the writer is reflective, ponders linguistic and ideational choices, is given to lapses of thought, is easily captivated by an idea or by the play of language) [and "might tend to produce discourse slowly" (79)].

2. The analytic style (the writer is cautious, precise, prefers a focus on the particulars of language or process rather than on the entire writing task) [and "might tend to get caught up in sentence-level particulars at the expense of broad discourse goals" (79)].

3. The pragmatic style (the writer tends to make interpretive and compositional choices in light of the purpose of the task—the writer looks outward to audience).[6]

Writer's Block and Writing Apprehension

For diagnostic work, Mike Rose's studies of writer's block are particularly helpful, for writer's block can stifle seemingly capable writers and cause them great difficulties. "I don't like to write" may be merely the surface expression of the real problem, "It takes me too long to write anything." And that time element is really due to writer's block, which Rose defines as "an inability to begin or continue writing for reasons other than a lack of basic skill or commitment" (3). As Rose explains, writers may block for one or more of a variety of reasons:

1. The rules by which such writers guide their composing processes are rigid, inappropriately invoked, or incorrect. For example, such writers will proclaim that "you must always put your thesis statement at the end of your first paragraph" or that "good writers never use the verb 'to be.'"

2. These writers' assumptions about composing are misleading. For example, they may believe that the best writing comes with little toil.

3. These writers edit too early in the composing process. Such editing can be premature and antiproductive when the writer tends to it unduly in early or rough draft stages. (Rose's high blockers edited twice as often as low blockers.)

4. These writers lack appropriate planning and discourse strategies or rely on inflexible or inappropriate strategies.

5. These writers invoke conflicting rules, assumptions, plans, and strategies. For example, a high blocker may state that writers must avoid the passive and keep "I" out of reports. (For a study of such contradictory perceptions, misinformation, and half-truths, see "Contradictory Perceptions of Rules for Writing.")[7]

6. These writers evaluate their writing with inappropriate criteria or criteria inadequately understood.

While writer's block can keep writers from writing, a related problem, writing anxiety, accompanies a number of ineffective writing habits and processes. In his survey of the research on writing apprehension, John Daly notes studies that show that overly anxious writers dislike writing, have little confidence in their writing abilities, fear evaluation of their written products, are less able than their peers to handle personal expressive writing such as narratives or descriptions, and produce fewer words. They also tend to infer less about their audience, engage in less planning, and spend less time planning sentences, editing, and reworking their writing. A case study done by Cynthia Selfe offers a close look at how writing apprehension affected the composing processes of a highly apprehensive writer who procrastinated, had a limited repertoire of writing skills, and was unable to attack academic writing problems successfully.[8]

Methods for Observing Writers' Composing Processes

To diagnose writer's block, writing apprehension, and other cognitive processing problems that can affect writers, there are several approaches. For writing apprehension there is a twenty-six-item questionnaire, the Daly-Miller Writing Apprehension Scale.[9] A method for uncovering writer's block suggested by Rose (86) is to gather students' writing histories by interviewing them—asking about previous writing courses, writing activities, and attitudes—and by examining every scrap of paper they used for a recent assignment. Yet another method is to observe students as they compose, a technique that lends itself well to the conference setting, for even watching a student compose a brief paragraph can be illuminating. Several methods for observing writing processes, discussed in more detail in "Diagnosing Writing Process Problems,"[10] are:

1. *Post hoc questioning:* Of the various observation methods, this is the least obtrusive, since it involves watching writers as they write and asking questions only afterward. Writers may not remember what they were thinking during various stages of composing and are prone to saying that they were engaged in what they think they should have been doing, but they still can report useful information about how they wrote.

2. *Stimulated recall:* This involves videotaping students as they write and playing back the tape as the writer comments on what was happening and responds to questions by the observer. As in post hoc questioning, the writer can forget or embellish, though the visual reminders on the videotape can help in triggering

more precise recall. (There is, of course, the problem of access to the necessary recording equipment.)

3. *Speaking-aloud protocols:* Here students are asked to verbalize aloud what they are thinking as they write. These protocols are taped and can be analyzed later. The intrusiveness of thinking aloud during composing is indeed a disturbance, and thinking aloud is, at best, an incomplete record because writers can say only some of what they are thinking. But despite these limitations, what is spoken is a very rich source of information.

In my work with speaking-aloud protocols used for diagnostic purposes, I have been able to observe students with a variety of composing process problems I would probably not have become aware of otherwise. In one case the student's well-written papers offered no clue as to why she found writing so difficult. Asked to discuss her problems, she could respond only with a symptom, that she spent many hours composing a few pages of text. Observation of her writing processes revealed that her difficulties sprang from indecisiveness— an inability to choose what to put on paper. Faced with options for content and word choice, she would generate yet more options and agonize over what to put on paper. Other students, asked to think aloud as they wrote, revealed other problems—of overdependence on the teacher's criteria rather than their own, of premature editing, of ineffective outlining, and of incessant rereading of the text being composed (these also are described more fully in "Diagnosing Writing Process Problems"). For those interested in using this method it is necessary to listen closely and to observe students' composing strategies as they write. Are the writer's strategies sufficiently varied, flexible, and complex? Do they help the writer complete the writing task appropriately? Are these strategies productive, or can we offer suggestions for improvement? Is there anything missing or inadequate in the student's composing processes? The answers to such questions can provide the kind of close, individualized help students need.

Cultural Differences

When our students are not members of the dominant American culture, there is yet another area of differentiation important for diagnostic work, that of culture. Students brought up in other cultures acquire habits, behavior patterns, perspectives, ways of delivering information, and other cultural filters that can affect writing in ways we often do not sufficiently attend to—and indeed are in danger of ignoring. For example, if another person's culture displays a strong preference for conveying information indirectly, merely criticizing paragraphs written in English by that person as too diffuse, wordy, or unclear is not likely to produce improvement. Instead, we must first recognize that we are dealing with a cultural difference and then discuss with that person the appropriate rhetorical patterns for prose in English.

That such differences abound is clear, for, as Robert Kaplan has noted, "Each language and each culture has a paragraph order unique to itself, and . . . part of the learning of a particular language is the mastering of its logical system."[11] In a later article Kaplan looks back at his earlier statements about the rhetorical structures of different languages and concludes that those earlier statements may have been too strongly worded.[12] But he still maintains that while all forms are possible in different languages, they don't occur with equal frequency. Such a statement reminds us not to form stereotypes about such cultural differences but, at the same time, to be aware of them as teachers, evaluators, and diagnosticians of writing. These students are not committing errors but employing a rhetoric and sequence of thought which are appropriate for them but which violate the expectations of a native English-speaking reader.

Kaplan's work on cultural thought patterns has defined for us the rhetorical structures of paragraphs and whole pieces of discourse— that is, how the text is organized and developed—for several languages. As Kaplan explains ("Cultural Thought Patterns," 4–9), English thought patterns are predominantly linear in development, allowing for little or no digression, while paragraph development in Semitic languages is based on a complex series of parallel constructions. Thus, maturity of style in English is often gauged by the degree of subordination rather than the coordination required in the extensive parallelism of a Semitic speaker's prose. In Karyn Thompson-Panos and Maria Thomas-Ruzic's analysis of Arabic, they note that coordinating conjunctions frequently appear at the beginning of Arabic sentences because of an Arabic predilection for emphasizing sequence of events and balance of thought, forms that favor coordination.[13] We might, therefore, see Arabic students' attempts to write English paragraphs as riddled with excessive *and*s and *but*s, as evident in the following excerpt from an Arab student's paper developed by coordination and parallelism:

> At that time of the year I was not studying enough to pass my courses in school. *And* all the time I was asking my cousin to let me ride the bicycle, *but* he wouldn't let me. *But* after two weeks, noticing that I was so much interested in the bicycle, he promised me that if I pass my courses in school for that year he would give

it to me as a present. *So* I began to study hard. *And* I studying eight hours a day instead of two.

My cousin seeing me studying that much he was sure that I was going to succeed in school. *So* he decided to give me some lessons in riding the bicycle. After four or five weeks of teaching me and ten or twelve times hurting myself as I used to go out of balance, I finally knew how to ride it. *And* the finals in school came *and* I was very good prepared for them *so* I passed them. My cousin kept his promise *and* gave me the bicycle as a present. *And* till now I keep the bicycle in a safe place, *and* everytime I see it, it reminds me how it helped to pass my courses for that year. (From Kaplan, "Cultural Thought Patterns," 9)

Since students from a Semitic culture will value this form of development, they need to learn not just how to subordinate in English but also why they should adopt patterns of expression they will not initially value as good writing.

Another difference in Arabic thought, noted by Edward Hall, is that history is used by Arabs as the basis for almost any modern action.[14] The chances are that an Arab won't start a talk or a speech or analyze a problem without first developing the historical aspect of his or her subject. Here again, we can imagine the response of a composition teacher, unaware of such a propensity, to a paper whose topic would not seem (to a native speaker of English) to require a historical perspective in the introduction. We can also imagine the Arab student's response when told that such an introduction is unnecessary or not to the point. Such a student might also be told that his or her writing is wordy and repetitious and perhaps too prone to overstatement because of stylistic differences which also mark Arabic prose. Thompson-Panos and Thomas-Ruzic (619) note that as part of the Arabic linguistic tradition main points are overasserted and exaggerated, thus calling for increased use of superlatives. Frequent rewording and restatement are also devices used for clarity of communication. Measured against the preferences of readers whose cultural conditioning leads them to favor moderation, understatement, and/or conciseness, typical Arabic structure and style may seem inadequate.

The prose of Oriental students, when evaluated in terms of rhetorical traditions taught in American schools, can appear deficient in other ways. After having taught in China, Carolyn Matalene warns us that some advice dispensed by Western teachers of writing is not easily understood by Chinese students learning English.[15] As Matalene explains, students trained in Chinese traditions absorb a cultural heritage that emphasizes memorization of phrases from classical sources and that values working within given traditions, not departing from them. To such students our recommendations that they avoid clichés and seek to use original phrases are counseling them "to write like uneducated barbarians" (792). In Kaplan's analysis ("Cultural Thought Patterns," 10), Oriental paragraphs are marked by indirection. The Oriental writer will circle around a subject, showing it from a variety of tangential views, but not looking at it directly. Development can be in terms of what things are not rather than what they are. For example, consider the following paragraphs written by a Korean student:

Definition of College Education

College is an institution of an higher learning that gives degrees. All of us needed culture and education in life, if no education to us, we should go to living hell.

One of the greatest causes that while other animals have remained as they first man along has made such rapid progress is has learned about civilization.

The improvement of the highest civilization is in order to education up-to-date.

So college education is very important thing which we don't need mention about it. (From Kaplan, "Cultural Thought Patterns," 10)

It is not uncommon in writing labs for Oriental students who have written such paragraphs to appear with notes from teachers asking for help in learning how to get to the point and to use more concrete details and examples. But merely giving these students such advice is not likely to effect much change if they continue to see the direct approach as rude. As one Oriental student admitted to me, "I would rather not offend my readers." Similarly, the Japanese preference, noted by Edward Hall, for going around and around a point can be frustrating to an American while the American preference for getting to the point so quickly is just as frustrating to the Japanese, who do not understand why Americans have to be so "logical" all the time.[16]

While Kaplan's analysis of cultural thought patterns concentrates heavily on Semitic and Oriental methods of development, he also notes that writers in French and Spanish exhibit much greater freedom to digress from their subjects than do writers in English. Kaplan offers the graphic representation in figure 1 of the movements of paragraphs from five different cultures.[17]

Although Kaplan reminds us that "much more detailed and more accurate descriptions are required before any meaningful contrastive systems can be elaborated" ("Cultural Thought Patterns," 15), his work can serve as an important reminder in our evaluation and diagnostic work that we cannot merely label as errors or problems those characteristics in the discourse of non-native speakers of English

English   Semitic   Oriental   Romance   Russian

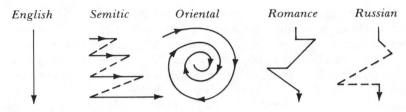

Figure 1.

which they bring with them from the rhetorical traditions of their own languages. Instead, we must realize the difficulty these students will have in trying to learn—and to accept as appropriate—cultural perspectives that may overturn or upset many of their unconscious assumptions about the world.

The depth to which cultural differences influence the content and development of written communication can also be seen in another factor, the degree of reader/writer involvement assumed by writers in different cultures. As explained by John Hinds, the concept of reader versus writer responsibility considers the degree of involvement the reader will have, a degree which will depend on the language being used.[18] In some languages, such as English, the writer (or speaker) is the person primarily responsible for effective communication, for making clear, well-organized statements. In other languages, however, such as Japanese, the reader (or listener) is the person primarily responsible, meaning that if a breakdown in communication occurs, it is the reader who assumes the burden of responsibility because he or she hasn't exerted enough effort. Muneo Yoshikawa's explanation for the Japanese view of reader responsibility is that because the Japanese mistrust verbal language what is not verbalized counts more than what is verbalized.[19] The Japanese reader/listener, who is supposed to know by "intuition" what is not said aloud, is therefore aware that what is expressed and what is actually intended are two different things. Similarly, Carolyn Matalene's study of Chinese rhetoric leads her to conclude that to be indirect, to expect the audience to infer meanings rather than to have them spelled out, is a defining characteristic of Chinese rhetoric.

A related perspective on the same cultural distinction is offered by Edward Hall, who differentiates between high-context and low-context cultures. It is typical of people in a high-context culture, Hall notes, to communicate less directly than do those in a low-context culture because they assume that much of what they think and mean can go without saying. This is possible in a high-context culture because of an extensive information network among family, friends, coworkers, and clients, who keep each other informed and reduce the need for context (or background information). Hall lists as examples of high-context cultures the French, Spanish, Italian, peoples of the Middle East, and Japanese. Examples of low-context cultures, notes Hall, are Americans and northern Europeans such as the Germans, Swiss, and Scandinavians. Thus, in intercultural communication, explains Hall, a German would seek detailed, explicit information, while a Japanese would be likely to feel uneasy if he or she were being too direct.[20] Because international business can suffer unless adjustments are made for different cultures, businesspeople are training themselves to become more aware of such differences. Similarly, as we read written communication from writers of other cultures, we too must be aware of such differences as we offer instruction and evaluate and diagnose papers. It is best, of course, to start by presenting these writers with the rhetorical information they need to write English prose, explaining not just the syntax and grammar of the language but its rhetorical standards and its readers' expectations as well. And we must be patient and realize that learning the intricacies of English verb tenses is still far easier than learning the role of the English-speaking reader.

The differences in reader/writer responsibility will also affect writing skills other than development and amount of information, since the distinction also impinges upon the unity of a text. English-speaking readers will, as Hinds explains, expect transition statements to be provided by the writer so that they can piece together the threads of the writer's logic. In Japanese discourse such landmarks may be absent or attenuated because it is the reader's responsibility to determine relationships between any one part of an essay and the essay as a whole. Transition statements do exist in Japanese, but Hinds characterizes them as more subtle and requiring a more active role on the reader's part, since it remains the reader's responsibility to create bridges. Edward Hall finds the same cultural perspective evident in the Japanese use of space, which illustrates what Hall describes as the Japanese "habit of leading the individual to a spot where he can discover something for himself." Hall also notes that in Arabic thinking, the conveyor of information is not responsible for building bridges because one is expected to connect widely separated points on his or her own, and very quickly too.[21]

Yet another writing skill, revision, can be affected by differences in reader/writer responsibility, for the inference drawn by Hinds from reader-responsible languages is that there is greater tolerance for ambiguity and imprecision of statement. While English-speaking writers go through draft after draft in order to produce a clear final product, Japanese authors frequently compose exactly one draft, which becomes the finished product. While this can hardly be equated with all reluctance to revise, Hinds's inference does serve to remind us that more generalized attitudes toward the world around us in different cultures can impinge upon writing processes. For example, Edward Hall notes that American Indians, who have a different sense of time, exhibit an indifference to finishing tasks all at once that is translated by whites as indolence. This is particularly true when the perceiver is a member of what Hall calls a monochronic culture, characterized by schedules, punctuality, and a sense that time forms a purposeful straight line. Typical monochronic people, says Hall, are Germans, Swiss, some other European cultures, and Americans. Rather than doggedly pursuing one task, as a person from a monochronic culture is likely to do, people in polychronic cultures, such as Hispanics, are comfortable with multiple tasks going on simultaneously and do not feel as constrained by deadlines and schedules.[22]

Only a few cultural distinctions that should concern us as writing teachers have been mentioned here, but it is clear that we need to be aware of such differences in our teaching and in our responses to students from other cultures. Yet much is still unknown about such differences. Hall estimates that the cultural systems that have never been made explicit probably outnumber explicit systems by a factor of one thousand or more.[23] The best we can do, then, is to be aware of how much we need to teach students from other cultures about the rhetorical expectations and standards of English discourse. And when their writing does not immediately seem to improve, we also have to realize the difficulty involved in adjusting to the mental frameworks that go with such new standards. It is not likely that these students can even verbalize for us the standards they have been using, for each system consists largely of what Hall calls "out-of-awareness" characteristics, the unconscious level of cultural norms. Every culture has a system, but the people who live by the system can tell others very little about its laws. As Hall points out, they can only tell you whether you are using the system correctly or not (*Beyond Culture*, 165–66). When someone is not using the system in English discourse, we can see from this discussion how that person's writing might be labeled as wordy, lacking in coherence, unfocused, unclear, or any of a number of other terms denoting writing problems at the rhetorical level. It is a challenge to our instructional skills to help these writers learn "the system" in English. The conference is a helpful place to do so, since we can keep probing and asking as we go to see how much each student understands of what we are explaining. The conference is also an excellent place to invite such students to discuss their feelings of bewilderment, confusion, and even embarrassment, as they try to conform to standards that are even more foreign than English vocabulary or the bewildering system of prepositions in English syntax.

The Written Product

Having considered two major components involved in diagnosis, the teacher and the student, we come now to what is the most familiar source of diagnostic information, the paper and the specific errors on the paper. Assessing written discourse is also an easier task because of the training many of us have had in analyzing prose and reviewing English grammar. With these tools we have the means to label strengths, weaknesses, and errors in student writing. Then, by listening, questioning, and observing the student, we can arrive at a diagnosis that determines what he or she needs to know.

For weaknesses in what Reigstad and McAndrew call "higher order concerns"[24] such as thesis, tone, organization, and development, or for other rhetorical concerns, such as purpose and audience awareness, we need to find out what the student intended and whether he or she has composing strategies adequate for the task. With this information, we can begin to formulate a plan of instruction suited to the particular student. A way into sorting through "lower order concerns" at the sentence and word levels is to hear the student read the paper aloud and separate out what the student can and cannot self-correct orally. For errors that the student recognizes and corrects, help with proofreading and editing is needed; for errors that the student corrects orally but doesn't recognize, help is needed in seeing what has been transcribed on the page. And, finally, for errors students cannot correct, we need to sort out patterns behind the labels, because mere labeling ("comma splice," "misplaced modifier," etc.) is relatively useless to students. Definitions of error can vary, and even if we were all to synchronize our definitions and labels, students would not suddenly learn to master rules that have evaded them for so long. What is needed, instead, is a sorting system that helps students look for types, systems, or groups of errors so that they can get a handle on what to do about them.

Error Analysis

This sorting of errors into types, known also as error analysis, can be illustrated in the following example of a student paragraph:

Mealtime

(1) Monday I ate in the cafateria for the first time. (2) I was not real sure what to do or where I should sit. (3) I only new one friend and he was getting a salad. (4) I wondered around for a few minutes and acted like I knew where I was going. (5) I finally asked him where he wanted to sit. (6) I also did not know how many servings I could take. (7) Eating the food was an other story. (8) Some things taste real good and other things are terrible. (9) The main course is usually alright but the side dishes need a little help. (10) The desserts are usually good though. (11) One thing I was not sure what to do was making a peanutbutter and jelly sandwich. (12) My friend said there was peanutbutter out there but I did not know where. (13) I also didn't know where the dishes where for the jello. (14) I know where most of the food is know but I am not planning on eating alot of the choices.

—John F.

A conversation with John, the author of this paper, might begin with his reading it aloud. While we cannot predict what he would correct on his own, it would be useful to hear if he stumbled over sentence 11 or tried to reword it. I suspect he would not correct any of the spelling errors or add any punctuation. In a writing lab, an opening question might be to ask John what his assignment was, to hear him verbalize the question he was answering in this paragraph. "We're supposed to write about something familiar" is the kind of unfocused response that would indicate why the purpose and point of the paper are so vague. An alternate question from John's classroom teacher would be a more direct question asking for his purpose and his point. Is John describing his first day in the cafeteria, giving a description of the cafeteria, or perhaps telling us how he learned to cope? This confusion may also exist in John's mind and would account for the sudden verb tense shift in sentences 8, 9, and 10 and the seeming digression on the general quality of the cafeteria food. At the sentence level, John's reliance on his spoken dialect probably accounts for the adverb/adjective problem in "real sure" and "real good." The various comma errors are all ones of omission, and we would need John's help in diagnosing the problem. Does he habitually ignore punctuation as unimportant, but if prompted could supply some needed commas? Or is he so unfamiliar with the rules that he cannot offer any suggestions for where to place commas? It would seem that John primarily needs to know how to punctuate compound sentences, but since he also needs to learn how to vary his sentence structures some sentence combining that included punctuation for the more commonly used patterns would solve two problems at once. Finally, John's spelling errors are mainly of one type, a confusion in transcribing his oral renderings. The type of spelling instruction to be provided would be aimed at helping John distinguish *new/knew, an other/another, know/now, wondered/wandered,* and *where/were*. The errors in "alright," "peanutbutter," and "alot" are also a matter of how to transcribe these sounds on paper. In addition, there is an unstressed vowel error in "cafateria," but since it is the only error of that type, a review of vowels seems unnecessary.

In David Bartholomae's classification of systematic errors, he notes three categories: (1) errors that are accidents, slips of the pen, as the writer's mind rushes ahead faster than his or her hand, (2) errors that are evidence of an intermediate system, a system being used by a student who has not yet acquired the accepted shorthand system of written English, and (3) errors of language transfer, or, more commonly, dialect interference, where in an attempt to produce the target language the writer intrudes forms from the first or native language (often a spoken dialect).[25] In John's paper we can see that many of his sentence-level errors fall within Bartholomae's third category of error, intrusions from spoken dialect, which would include John's spelling errors, overuse of coordination, and adverb/adjective confusion. That such errors are caused by the tendency of unskilled writers to resort to spoken language inappropriately is illustrated in James Collins's discussion of this major source of error in "Dialogue and Monologue and the Unskilled Writer."[26] Collins illustrates the problem with the following excerpt from a student paper:

> Pep rallies are supposed to build up school spirit to get the energy flowing through the blood and your Body. You get siked for the sport events for the foot Ball, Swimming, etc. You must be mentally and phisicly prepaired for a sport event.
> Then every Body runs of the bleacher and runs around and yells alot. "Were the Best" etc. then every Body goes home and then the sports events start and Nobody else cares but the jocks. (84)

Many of the errors noted by Collins in this paper are similar to those in John's paper in the previous example. In both, spellings are accomplished through sound or through analogy with similar-sounding words, and in both students' writing the sentences are juxtaposed, run together, or connected loosely with overworked conjunctions such as "and" and "but." An additional characteristic that Collins notes in the second paper, that meaning is abbreviated (as in the use of "etc.") as if the reader were a partner in a dialogue, is not quite as evident in John's paper, but is certainly a problem there too.

Another cause of error at the sentence level, identified by Colette Daiute, is the limitation of short-term memory during composing.[27]

In Daiute's study of the relationship between performance on short-term memory tests for sentences and the ability to write grammatical sentences, the results showed that writers with relatively low scores on tests of short-term memory ability for sentences wrote more sentences with errors than did subjects with higher short-term memory scores. Daiute's taxonomy of errors, the result of her analysis of 450 syntax errors written by college students, includes twelve apparently different types of syntax problems. These errors occur immediately after a previous clause has been encoded on the page, on the average after about eleven words have been written. As an example, Daiute includes the following sentence:

> I really enjoyed flying in an airplane that I understand how
> it works. (8)

In Daiute's analysis, the first sentence the writer composed, "I really enjoyed flying in an airplane that I understand," overlapped with "I understand how it works." This overlapping occurred, explains Daiute, because the writer did not hold the first clause in mind exactly as it was worded, so the memory of its syntactic form faded as the second clause was encoded. Other errors that Daiute notes as due to performance constraints on memory include the following:

1. Fragments ("Because the type of training a child gets from the computer is nothing compared to playing.")

2. Distant modifier sentence ("The children were driven away in buses with big windows laughing and singing.")

3. Nonparallel sentence ("The main purpose of government is representation and to protect the rights of citizens.")

4. Gapped sentence ("Mechanical devices have tendency to lose student's attention.")

5. Repetitious sentence ("Your achievement in life can be very good in life but every American does not want to do a lot of work.")

6. Multi-error sentence ("Most important to me is self-satisfaction of myself and the family that I have, without one is not successful.")

Another type of error, one that occurs with great frequency, appears in the following example, offered by Robert de Beaugrande: "You see I'm trying to avoid another scrambled egg breakfast. Basically because I hate them."[28] De Beaugrande's explanation of the type of fragment in the second sentence is that it is formulated as an adjunct whose core is in an adjacent sentence, generally the preceding one (as it is here), but sometimes the following one. De Beaugrande speculates that such fragments may occur because of time lags as conceptual or phrasal chunks are returned by memory search, because their format roughly resembles a sentence, or because they are long and complex (248–49). In "Mending the Fragmented Free Modifier" I've offered another possible cause for this very common form of fragment, that it occurs as students reach for more mature sentence patterns, including free modifiers and modification before and after the main clause, but are unaware of the correct punctuation for such patterns.[29] Asked why they inserted periods in such sentences, students have told me, "The sentence was getting too long" or, "I know it needed some punctuation because I could hear the break."

As for another frequent sentence-level error, comma splices, de Beaugrande suggests that they be remedied in view of their causes. One cause, explains de Beaugrande, is the relatedness of two statements, with the second usually giving support or elaboration to the first. Another cause can be the confusion between clause-linking junctures and adverbials.[30] Helen Ewald also notes that comma splices tend to occur when the subject of the second clause is a pronoun.[31]

One of the challenges of error analysis is for the researcher to gather together seemingly disparate errors which can be explained (and treated) by reference to a common cause. Such is the result of a study done by F. J. Sullivan and Donald C. Freeman, who concluded that when writers lack a sense of agency (who or what is acting on someone or something else), the writing can suffer from a whole list of difficulties, including passives without clear agents, infinitives and gerunds without clear underlying subjects, vague pronouns, subject-verb agreement errors, faulty parallelism, and misrelated modifiers. As an example of an unclear gerund, Sullivan and Freeman offer the following sentence and a revised version which clarifies the agent:

> Example: Editing, cutting, and being able to alter the finished product are only a few examples of the technical superiority that a movie has over a play.

> Revision: Because a film director can edit, cut, and alter the finished product, a movie is technically superior to a play.[32]

Their revision restores the agent, the film director, to the sentence, for it is the director, not the movie, who edits, cuts, and alters. Similarly, the subject-verb error in the next sentence is removed when the agent is clarified:

> Example: The finished movie with all its corrections and adjustments help to make the movie as perfect as possible.

> Revision: As the director corrects and adjusts in finishing the movie, he can make the final product as perfect as possible. (146)

One more example, of faulty parallelism, indicates how lack of an agent can create errors and vague writing:

> Example: The camera can fool the human eye, and in conjunction with make-up and costuming makes for a much more enjoyable performance.

> Revision: We enjoy movies more than we do plays because of the greater visual effects of make-up, costuming, and camera techniques, which can fool the human eye. (147)

Second Language Interference

For students learning English as a second language, there is another source of error included in Bartholomae's taxonomy that we need to be aware of, namely interference from another language, the carrying over of patterns and forms from the student's first language into English. Although contrastive analysis, the comparison of the systems of one language with those of another, is no longer used as a foundation for instructional programs, it can be a useful tool for understanding typical sentence-level mistakes and problems that occur among students acquiring English. For example, the particular difficulty Oriental students have with remembering to use articles is due, in part, to the lack of such markers in their language. Similarly, the tendency of Spanish-speaking students to write overly long sentences in English can be understood in light of the length of typical sentences in Spanish. Among Arab students, Thompson-Panos and Thomas-Ruzic (615) have noted the omission of forms of "to be" (as in "My teacher angry") because the surface structure of Arabic has no such copula. Arab students are also likely to experience difficulty with relative clauses because there is no relative pronoun in Arabic. And Arabic- and Hebrew-speaking students may omit vowels in their spelling because in their languages vowels are often omitted in written transcriptions of words. We may also notice that some non-native students are not good dictionary users and will need help in becoming familiar with how English dictionaries work. Arabic dictionaries, for example, are difficult for users because words are entered under their roots. Thompson-Panos and Thomas-Ruzic (613) compare this to looking up the English word "misconceived" under the root "cept." Other languages interfere in other ways, and while we cannot be expected to be aware of all the differences and similarities between the

languages our students speak and English, it is helpful to stop sometimes and ask the student how his or her language compares to
English for whatever matter is under discussion. It may give us an
insight into the difficulty the student is having or may serve as the
springboard for a more useful discussion about how the student can
acquire the English rule needed. Typically, we can expect students
learning English as a second language to experience difficulties with
the errors noted by Mark LeTourneau: inflection of nouns, verbs, and
adverbs; count and non-count nouns (those which can be counted and
have plurals and those which cannot); prepositions; tenses; definite
articles; and word order.[33] But we can also expect that every language
has the potential for interfering in unexpected ways with attempts to
master English.

Learning Disabilities

Another area for diagnostic consideration, one beyond the scope of this
book, is that of learning disabilities, particularly dyslexia. Dyslexia is
a condition too complex—and some would say as yet too little
understood—to deal with briefly. But we need to consider the possibility that some of our students need more help than we are able to
provide and that we might need to refer them, if possible, to professionals in the field of learning disabilities. Symptoms to watch for
include poor handwriting in which the writer tends to fuse adjacent
letters into one and several types of spelling errors, including two
types noted by Andrew W. Ellis in *Reading, Writing, and Dyslexia:
A Cognitive Analysis*.[34] Some errors in the writing of dyslexics,
Ellis notes, are phonic, as in "gowing" for "going" or "ecode" for
"echoed," but a great many others, when pronounced, would not
sound like the target words. Included in this second category would be
letters in the wrong order ("thrid" for "third" or "pakr" for "park")
and spellings which indicate retrieval of only partial information
from the speller's graphemic word production system ("mechinal" for
"mechanical"). An example of such writing might look like figure 2.
Other identifying features of dyslexic students, described by David
Taylor, include oral reading which is hesitant and inaccurate, with
inattention to punctuation, mispronunciation of known words, omission of short words, and substitution of incorrect words for others
with similar configurations. Taylor also notes that dyslexics' written
vocabulary often seems limited because of an inability to spell all the
words they know.[35] We can offer such students help with spelling,
proofing, and general transcription skills, but we cannot expect that
their progress will equal the effort they expend.

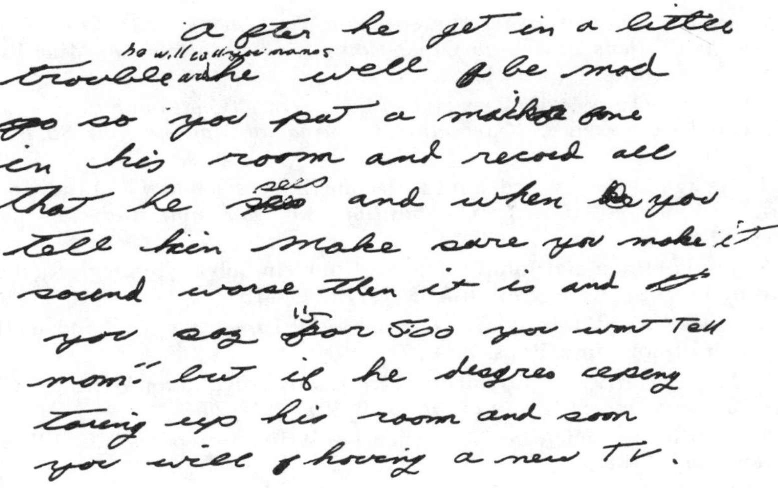
after he get in a littel
so will call you names
troublea he well of be mad
so so you put a maike one
in his room and record all
that he sees and when you
tell him make sure you make it
sound worse then it is and
you say for soo you wont Tell
mom: but if he degrees ceping
toring up his room and soon
you will of having a new TV.

Figure 2.

Conclusion

Diagnosis, like writing, is a bit of a juggling act, for we must keep numerous considerations in focus simultaneously. As we seek out what it is that will help the writer progress, we should keep in mind our own propensities and preferences, the student's individual makeup and history, and the array of symptoms on the page. And, like writing, diagnosis is an ongoing process as we keep exploring with students what is best for their development. One-shot attempts at diagnosis are usually no closer to successful end products than are first drafts of writing, but the exploration process is not—as in writing—performed by one person. Both the student and the teacher work together to move forward, and it is in the conference conversation that all of the back-and-forth motion, discussion, questions, and suggestions come up. This kind of diagnosis, so much richer than the mere act of labeling error (which we call "paper grading"), is a complex, but rewarding, aspect of what conferences can offer students as they develop their writing skills.

Notes

1. William F. Irmscher, review of *The Writer's Mind: Writing as a Mode of Thinking,* ed. Janice N. Hays, Phyllis A. Roth, Jon R. Ramsay, and Robert D. Foulke, *College Composition and Communication* 35 (1983): 369.

2. John A. Daly, "Writing Apprehension," in *When a Writer Can't Write: Studies in Writer's Block and Other Composing Problems,* ed. Mike Rose (New York: Guilford, 1985), 43–82.

3. See, for example, G. Pask and B. C. E. Scott, "Learning Strategies and Individual Competence," *International Journal of Man-Machine Studies* 4 (1972): 217–53.

4. George H. Jensen and John K. DiTiberio, "Personality and Individual Writing Processes," *College Composition and Communication* 35 (1984): 285–300.

5. Linda Flower and John R. Hayes, "Problem-Solving Strategies and the Writing Process," *College English* 35 (1977): 449–61.

6. Mike Rose, *Writer's Block: The Cognitive Dimension* (Carbondale, Ill.: Southern Illinois Univ. Press, 1984), 78.

7. Muriel Harris, "Contradictory Perceptions of Rules for Writing," *College Composition and Communication* 30 (1979): 218–20.

8. Cynthia L. Selfe, "An Apprehensive Writer Composes," in *When a Writer Can't Write.*

9. John A. Daly and M. Miller, "The Empirical Development of an Instrument to Measure Writing Apprehension," *Research in the Teaching of English* 9 (1975): 242–49.

10. Muriel Harris, "Diagnosing Writing Process Problems: A Pedagogical Application of Speaking-Aloud Protocol Analyses," in *When a Writer Can't Write,* 166–81.

11. Robert B. Kaplan, "Cultural Thought Patterns in Inter-Cultural Education," *Language Learning* 16 (1966): 14.

12. Robert B. Kaplan, "Cultural Thought Patterns Revisited," in *Analyzing Writing: Models and Methods,* ed. Ulla Connor and Robert B. Kaplan (Reading, Mass.: Addison-Wesley, forthcoming).

13. Karyn Thompson-Panos and Maria Thomas-Ruzic, "The Least You Should Know about Arabic: Implications for the ESL Writing Instructor," *TESOL Quarterly* 17 (1983): 620.

14. Edward T. Hall, *The Silent Language* (New York: Doubleday, 1959), 172.

15. Carolyn Matalene, "Contrastive Rhetoric: An American Writing Teacher in China," *College English* 47 (1985): 792.

16. Edward T. Hall, *The Hidden Dimension* (Garden City, N.Y.: Doubleday, Anchor Press, 1969), 151.

17. Kaplan, "Cultural Thought Patterns," 15.

18. John Hinds, "Reader versus Writer Responsibility: A New Typology," in *Analyzing Writing.*

19. Summarized in Hinds.

20. Quoted in Gary Blonston, "The Translator," *Science 85* 6, no. 6 (1985): 84.

21. Hall, *Hidden Dimension,* 154.

22. Quoted in Blonston, 82–84.

23. Edward T. Hall, *Beyond Culture* (Garden City, N.Y.: Doubleday, Anchor Press, 1977), 165–66.

24. Thomas J. Reigstad and Donald A. McAndrew, *Training Tutors for Writing Conferences* (Urbana, Ill.: ERIC Clearinghouse on Reading and Communication Skills and National Council of Teachers of English, 1984).

25. David Bartholomae, "The Study of Error," *College Composition and Communication* 31 (1980): 253–69.

26. James C. Collins, "Dialogue and Monologue and the Unskilled Writer," *English Journal* 71 (Apr. 1982): 84–86.

27. Colette A. Daiute, "Psycholinguistic Foundations of the Writing Process," *Research in the Teaching of English* 15 (1981): 5–22.

28. Robert de Beaugrande, *Text Production: Toward a Science of Composition* (Norwood, N.J.: Ablex, 1984), 248–49.

29. Muriel Harris, "Mending the Fragmented Free Modifier," *College Composition and Communication* 28 (1981): 175–82.

30. de Beaugrande, 252.

31. Helen Rothschild Ewald, "Using Error Analysis in the Writing Lab for Correctness and Effectiveness," *Writing Lab Newsletter* 8, no. 5 (1984): 6–8.

32. F. J. Sullivan and Donald C. Freeman, "The Interaction of Agency and Affect in Diagnosing and Remedying Syntactic Errors," Temple University Working Papers in Composition (Philadelphia: Dept. of English, Temple University, n.d.), 145.

33. Mark LeTourneau, "Typical ESL Errors and Tutoring Strategies," *Writing Lab Newsletter* 9, no. 7 (1985): 5–8.

34. Andrew W. Ellis, *Reading, Writing, and Dyslexia: A Cognitive Analysis* (Hillsdale, N.J.: Lawrence Erlbaum Associates, 1984).

35. David Taylor, "Identifying and Helping the Dyslexic Writer," *Journal of Developmental Education* 9, no. 2 (1985): 8–11.

5 Strategies for Teaching
   One-to-One

The basic assumption of this book is that the one-to-one setting of the conference is a superb teaching environment. But that does not mean that putting a student and a teacher together will automatically result in better teaching and more learning. No mystical transformation takes place: ineffective teachers can remain ineffective; recalcitrant, indifferent, or slow learners can remain recalcitrant, indifferent, or slow. What the conference does provide is a setting where a different—and some of us would say better—kind of teaching can take place. Every chapter of this book has dealt with some aspect of these differences, such as the possibility for effective interaction, individualized feedback and diagnosis, and so on; and here we will be concerned with yet another difference, specific teaching strategies that are appropriate to the conference setting.

Since teachers differ as much in their theoretical approaches and teaching styles as students differ in their writing habits and problems, this chapter offers not a definitive set of "how tos" but a grab bag for teachers and tutors to dip into, a collection of strategies from which to draw something useful. One teacher's strategy cannot automatically be used by another because strategies have to fit not only different teaching styles and personalities but also different theoretical or pedagogical preferences. We also have to consider students' own differences, in their learning styles, in their problems, and in the sources or causes of those problems.

The notion of a grab bag, then, implies that all of us can select what looks useful for ourselves and switch from one strategy to another when the first one doesn't work. We might find ourselves working with one student who finds visual representations helpful, while for another having us call attention to an error several times helps in proofreading for it. The teacher's flexibility in moving on and trying something different is a key factor in the success of conferences. That "moving on" is the result of the kind of ongoing diagnosis discussed in chapter 4. It is the interaction of teacher and student, the teacher checking to see how things are working and the student offering the immediate feedback needed in that checking, that determines the forward motion of a conference.

To provide an indication of the variety of approaches we can use in conferences, this chapter will first offer some strategies for helping students with rhetorical and composing skills. The rest of the chapter offers some general strategies for dealing with grammatical errors and then some techniques that help students improve their editing skills when dealing with specific problems in sentence structure, punctuation, spelling, usage, and all the other matters covered under the general rubric of "grammar."

Strategies for Working on Rhetorical and Composing Skills

For teachers, the conference provides the necessary opportunity to hear writers talk about their writing, to listen to their intentions, and to help them lessen the disparity between what was attempted and what was achieved. And that help may involve assistance with any one of a number of writing skills, including those listed here.

Planning, Generating, and Developing

When students come to conferences before they begin a piece of writing, they may be at the very early stages of choosing a general subject. If there are no constraints of any kind on choosing a topic, they may flounder in so much freedom and need help locating areas of interest. "What should I write about?" is a dead-end question students pose for themselves, a question that we need to rephrase because it provokes no purpose in the writer's mind and stirs no urge to communicate to an audience. Instead, we might ask, "If I were to write a biographical sketch of you, what would you like me to write?" or, "Suppose I were interviewing you for the newspaper and wanted to question you on one of your favorite topics. What would I ask questions about?" Peer tutors I have overheard have great success with questions such as "If we were going to meet at a party and I asked a friend of yours what you liked to talk about, what would your friend suggest?" Or, we might ask, "What have you been thinking or reading about lately?" or inquire about personal interests or goals. For term paper topics, a helpful leading question is "What would you like to learn more about?" Additional subjects might be suggested through profile questionnaires which ask students to discuss aspects of their personal history and views about themselves and their world.[1]

Sometimes students have trouble locating their own topics within a general subject that has been assigned. Asked to write about meaningful experiences in their lives, memorable persons they have known, special holiday celebrations in their families, and so on, some students need assistance in making subjects come alive for them. One approach is to start swapping stories; if we offer them something that we might write about, as in any conversational setting some students will respond with their own stories. Another approach is to ask students merely to rattle off several possibilities that anyone (not necessarily they) might write about, a type of brainstorming technique but less threatening because the writer is not being asked to generate a topic for his or her own paper. That is, students may not initially be able to choose a memorable person they would care to write about, but most can begin generating a list of possibilities. It helps considerably for us to contribute to the growing list, a sort of "think tank" approach in which one person's ideas help initiate more ideas in the other person. When there is an adequate list of possibilities, it's easier to begin to narrow and focus than it was initially to come up with a single topic.

When a subject has been chosen, student and teacher can turn their attention to purpose and audience. The teacher's role here is not only as a listener but also as a recorder, keeping brief notes (or memory jogs) as students talk and explore what they might write about. Any of the heuristic questions offered in composition texts can keep the conversation flowing forward as the student goes on to generate material; but for some teachers, invention probes such as looping, cubing, tagmemics, the journalistic W's (who, what, when, where, why, how), the pentad, and so on are less useful than the simple invitation, "Tell me more." Sometimes we can serve as useful aids to a student's invention just by being an interested audience asking whatever questions any listener in need of more information might ask.

Linda Flower and John Hayes's strategies for generating ideas include the process of "playing your thoughts," a process that can include brainstorming, staging a scenario (role playing), playing out an analogy (this topic is like X), and allowing oneself time to rest and incubate. To push the ideas generated through any or all of these processes, that is, to develop more material, Flower and Hayes offer several strategies: (1) find a cue word or rich bit (a word which taps into a network of ideas and associations in the writer's mind), (2) nutshell the ideas and teach them (which forces the writer both to summarize the major focus and also to elaborate in order to be sure that listeners will get the point), (3) tree the ideas (which involves putting the fragments of brainstorming into a hierarchical order of some kind, but not necessarily an outline), and (4) test the writing by reading as if you were the reader.[2]

Focusing on a Thesis or Main Point

When a writer has generated material and has either a rough draft or enough planning notes to begin defining a specific point or focus for a paper, the give and take of a conference dialogue can help him or her arrive at a workable thesis statement. Sometimes being asked to verbalize the point to someone else is sufficient to help students arrive at their preferred main idea. Straightforward questions such as "What point do you want to make?" or "If I walked up to your desk and asked what you're writing about, what would you say?" are helpful here. Then we need to listen while students formulate their responses to such questions.

We can again help writers by taking a few notes, if possible, about what they are saying while they talk, because in the process of formulating or considering various options they may forget some of what they have generated. I've noticed my note taking to be particularly helpful for students who are weighing options for difficult word choices in their thesis statements. The cognitive effort expended on each choice seems to drive the previous one from short-term memory, but seeing their options on paper helps their recall and frees such students from having to remember previous options while simultaneously generating new ones. Taking notes for students is also helpful when they inadvertently shift their points as they formulate various drafts of their statements. Noting a shift, disparity, or drift is easier when the options are caught on paper and can be compared visually. When we record student versions of a main point on paper, we may also be demonstrating writing behavior some students haven't yet tried.

Another prompt to help students formulate their points is the one used by Robert Child in his tutorials, as he writes down and explains the following:[3]

thesis = promise

I promise that I will talk about _____ in this (or these) ways

_____

_____

_____

The particular way in which the instructor formulates the original question or offers the above strategy is of less importance than the dialogue that follows. We can listen, ask appropriate questions, keep notes, and help students realize strengths and weaknesses in their formulations of their topic sentences. Are they promising to take on too much in a short paper (e.g., "the causes of international terrorism" or "a condemnation of current television"), or have they not yet defined their terms or the approach they'll take (e.g., "Surgery can be dangerous to your health" or "I like my house")? Sometimes it is helpful during the middle stages of formulating a main point to turn away from the sentence being worked on and to some sample thesis statements not originated by the student, and to criticize these together. Some textbooks (e.g., chapter 6 in *Practice for a Purpose*) have such exercises in criticizing thesis statements that are vague, too broad, or too limited.

Sometimes a student will appear in a conference with a draft that has several possibilities for a focus, as is evident in paper 3, Fran's paper, in appendix B, part 3. In this paper, the writer starts out by introducing one topic, the rigors of Nordic skiing, and then moves on to a description of the glories of the Colorado landscape and our need to "return to the land and discover our essential elements." As a first draft, this is a promising piece of writing, but the writer needs to see that she has drifted from one topic to another. One method for helping her is to provide reader feedback, that is, to read the paper and offer a running summary of what we are reading as we proceed and what our expectations as readers are. This is more effective when we read the paper "cold" for the first time, so that the student knows she is getting unrehearsed, spontaneous reactions. Our running commentary on this paper might proceed as follows:

> At the end of the first paragraph: "I can see that this paper is going to tell me about the rigors of Nordic skiing. I've heard that it's hard, and now I can find out how hard it really is."
>
> At the end of the second paragraph: "Well, Nordic skiing does sound difficult. You've described the sweat you work up, the strain on your muscles, the gasping for breath, and the sting of the snowflakes. Doesn't exactly sound like an after-lunch stroll!"
>
> After a few sentences of the third paragraph: "This description of the Rockies is interesting, but I thought I was going to hear more about the difficulties of Nordic skiing."
>
> At the beginning of the last paragraph (after the first sentence or so): "Hmmm, I'm getting lost here. I thought I was reading about Nordic skiing, and then I found myself immersed in a description of the Rockies, and now I seem to be in the middle of a discussion of our need to maintain contact with the natural world."

A student watching and listening to a reader moving along and commenting in some manner similar to the above can *see* the topic drift. The student's task then is to decide which of these possible topics will be the main focus for the next draft. Or the student may have a larger topic in mind that includes much of what is contained in this draft, but the larger topic and the threads of connection have not been established for the reader. For example, in Fran's paper, she may have wanted to use the physical exertion of her sport and the beauties of the Colorado landscape in some way to bring us to a deeper sense of what is involved in her concept of returning to the land. But until Fran clarifies her thinking on paper, we as readers have no way of knowing her real topic. Offering her a reader's feedback on the realization of her point and comparing that to a statement of her intention is a way into working on the disparity between the two.

Drafts of other papers present different variations on this problem. For example, as a reader of Traci's paper (number 10 in appendix B, part 3), I might tell the writer that I seem to be getting two somewhat different points from the paper, that spring break vacations are expensive and that such Florida vacations are worthless (leaving students with little "besides a Florida tan and a few t-shirts"). I might ask which one she intended to emphasize.

A somewhat different approach, that of Peter Elbow's "believing game,"[4] is useful when a draft has a seemingly ill-defined, vague, trite, or ineffective thesis that some unsympathetic readers might pounce on (the "I'd-rather-read-the-phone-book" syndrome). Such papers have topics such as "My puppy is my friend," "Small towns are boring," or "Autumn is my favorite season." When we as readers are faced with such papers, Elbow suggests that we try the believing game, that is, that we try as hard as we can to believe that the statement being made is true. If we do, we can help writers push through and see why they have made such declarations. Elbow asks us to make an effort "to believe assertions that are hard to believe or give richness and power to ideas that may seem thin" because if we do, we may "even notice something true or useful about the idea that its supporters hadn't noticed since we come freshly to it with a contrasting frame of mind or 'set' " (341–42). This technique is particularly useful for teachers who, as Elbow explains, naturally resist the believing game because we have had to learn to be doubters, accepting only what cannot be doubted.

Organizing Drafts

When students need help with organizing, they may be having difficulties in seeing the lack of organization in a draft, or they may realize what they need to do but not have any useful strategies for doing it. For short papers, organization is often a second step, imposing order on early drafts and explorations. Helping a student gain the high ground, to see an overview of what is there, can be a matter of working with him or her to map out segments of the paper. Textbook-style outlines aren't necessary (and tend to look a bit rigid and forbidding), but whatever tree diagram, map, sketch, or list is made should show coordination and subordination of ideas. Thus a simple sketch that can be made in a brief conference might look like figure 3. We can work with a student to produce a quick list or sketch of some form by using prompts such as "What's your first paragraph about? . . . What's your second paragraph about? . . . What else is in that paragraph? How is that part of what you said the paragraph was about?"

For students unfamiliar with ways to develop an overview of a paper, we help by initially being note takers as they talk, to show them how before turning over to them the responsibility for recording a few notes of what they say. Once a sketch or list is on paper, we can look at the arrangement together, helping students to consider others that are potentially more effective, to note sections that don't seem to belong, or to see repetitions of ideas from one paragraph to another. For example, in Eric's paper (2 in appendix B, part 3), a visual diagram would help him see that the opening sentence of the second paragraph (which doesn't pertain to the rest of the paragraph) is the same as the opening statement of the third paragraph and that a part

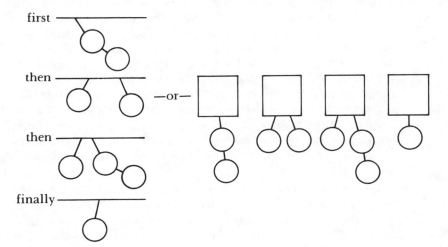

Figure 3.

of the fifth paragraph repeats a point made in the second paragraph. The relevant parts of the list would be as follows:

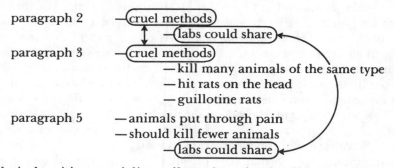

Technical writing specialists tell us that visuals (diagrams, charts, and so on) are more effective in communicating certain ideas than prose, and this is certainly the case if we compare the laborious explanation of the lack of organization in Eric's paper given above to the visual demonstration.

Using Specific Details

When a paper is too general and needs more specific details, there are several ways we can help the writer see its effect on the reader:

1. As we progress through the paper, we can suggest some of the different possibilities that may occur to us as readers. For example, when a student writes, "Terry was my special friend because we always had fun together," the reader might explain, "I'm not sure what kind of fun you mean here. I think that grooming a horse for a show is fun. Is this the kind of fun you mean?" Or "They played some great music" can prompt the following set of questions about possible meanings: "Was the music great because it was new music you had never heard? Was it great because you liked the electronic percussion sound, or was it, perhaps, great because you could sing along?" When faced with a few choices that could occur to readers, a writer can begin to see the need to narrow these choices by using more specific language.

2. Sometimes a generalization in need of details can be called to the writer's attention with a simple question like, "Can you give me an example here?" Telling the writer how much that example helps us to follow along reinforces the value of examples for readers.

3. Another conference strategy for helping writers use more descriptive detail, offered by Peter Schiff, involves having teacher and writer revise each other's writing. They begin with about five minutes of free-writing and then exchange drafts so that each can suggest areas for possible expansion in the other's writing through the use of specific examples and details.[5]

4. If lack of detail is more than just an occasional problem in the paper, we can stop and practice the use of details with examples offered as practice in some textbooks (e.g., chapter 7 in *Practice for a Purpose*).

5. As a rather drastic illustration, the teacher who first read John's paper (6 in appendix B) reread the paper aloud to John, substituting "constructing jigsaw puzzles" everywhere that John had written "building model cars." The lack of specificity that allows such interchangeability can be a vivid demonstration for writers that they need to nail down their topics with particulars.

Checking for Transitions and Coherence

When student writing lacks coherence or adequate transitions between ideas, there are a variety of ways that students, teachers, and textbooks describe the results. Students who sense something missing might describe the paper as "choppy" or say that it doesn't "flow." Teachers might also use such terms, or they might take the reader's perspective and see a lack of audience awareness or lack of information as the problem. This inability to conceptualize the audience's need for information is seen as symptomatic of the immature writer who has not yet decentered, that is, realized the "otherness" of readers. James Collins describes this in somewhat different terms. He explains that unskilled writers, regardless of age or grade level, produce writing marked by features of spoken dialogue.[6] Their writing seems to assume reader familiarity with contexts of situation and culture; that is, they assume that readers, like participants in a dialogue where there is a mutual process of constructing meaning, share referential contexts. When we write, however, the process is solitary, a monologue in which no sharing in the construction of meaning takes place. Students who fail to realize this distinction and continue to talk on paper construct essays that can mystify readers because of inadequate explanation.

Collins's strategy for making writers aware of this problem is to show them how confused we can be as readers when there is a lack of information. Walker Gibson also advises us to play the dumb reader, to respond to signals on the page, to let students see what readers ignorant of writers' intentions will make of the text.[7] When the writer has seen this, the teacher and writer can backtrack together to see where the "dumb reader" went wrong. What we are really searching for here is where the writer went wrong in failing to set up signals that would have kept the reader going down the intended path.

Gibson calls this failure to set up signals a failure of imagination on the writer's part, but there may be other reasons that information is omitted. Some students, if asked to characterize their audience, describe the reader as smarter than they are and therefore less in need of information. When a student's career as a writer has been to compose primarily for the teacher as reader, the "all-knowing teacher" becomes the writer's abstract concept of audience. Fear of redundancy can be another cause for omitted information. Students who have been drilled on ridding their papers of repetition can even become hesitant to restate information used in the paper's title.

Playing the dumb reader, or explaining that readers are not as smart as writers think they are, is a method for helping writers become aware of this problem. A similar conference strategy is to read the paper with the writer and give him or her feedback on what we are getting from the text. In the excerpt from Mickey's tutorial in appendix A, the tutor is doing this, telling the writer what is being understood and asking questions about what is unclear. As readers, we can also anticipate for the student what we think will be coming next. This might be particularly helpful in the paper written by Janet (5 in appendix B). At the end of the introductory paragraph, when Janet offers her main point ("There should be more punishment for criminals in the United States"), we could tell the writer that we expect the next paragraph to deal with some aspect of punishment for criminals, perhaps discussing what is meant by "more punishment" or offering reasons that there should be more punishment. When the next paragraph moves instead into a discussion of how criminals can harm their victims, we can compare for Janet the difference between normal reader expectation and the actual text. Janet needs to see that without drawing threads of connection, she can confuse her readers by this seeming shift in direction.

When students need transitions between sentences, we can ask as we read, "How will this next sentence be related to the one we just read?" If there is a handy list of transition words and devices to refer to, students can browse through it for suggestions. A visual representation of this process of linking sentence to sentence is the diagram Robert Child draws for a student having trouble conceptualizing the problem. Child asks his student to consider an essay as an electrical current, with extension cords that must be plugged into each other. Every time there is a missing plug, the reader is lost because of the breakdown. Child's drawings tend to look like figure 4.

As an example, Child offers an exaggerated case, such as the following, in which there is a mysterious leap to "Of course" in the last sentence, making the connection difficult for the reader.

> I'm going to town this afternoon to buy some [soda]. While I'm there, I think I'll also get some peanuts. Of course, I'll have to go to the bank first.

A metaphor that works for some students who are unsure of methods for hooking paragraphs together is the crochet hook (a metaphor which, of course, works only for those with some vague knowledge of crocheting). Just as the crochet hook reaches up to pull a thread from above down to the next row, so too can the writer reach up for a reference to the previous paragraph in the opening of the next paragraph.

Revising

Revising, of course, is done for a variety of purposes, throughout the writing of a paper. Thus in this chapter we have already reviewed matters that concern the writer at any stage of writing, from early drafting to later revising. Because revising goes on constantly, it is difficult to isolate specific concerns that can be labeled as matters of revising, beyond what has already been discussed. But there are some matters that many writers leave for subsequent passes through a paper, the kind of polishing concerned with pervasive matters such as tone, style, voice, or word-level matters of diction. Reader feedback in the conference is particularly helpful with such concerns.

For matters of tone, style, and voice (terms that for some teachers are a string of synonyms and for others are very different matters), we

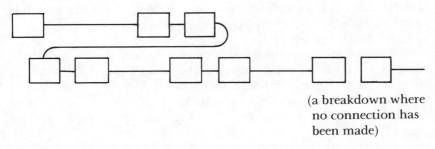

(a breakdown where no connection has been made)

Figure 4.

can offer writers help by giving them our reactions as readers. Discussing those reactions in the privacy and informality of a conference can easily lead to discussions of options for revision. While some teachers and tutors achieve considerable success with this kind of close response to the student's text, David Kaufer's work on developing computer tutorials has led him to suggest that for this kind of revision, we draw back and begin at a very general level, asking only leading questions such as "Do you really talk like that?" or "Does this sound stilted to you?" Kaufer's principle here is never to give away more than you have to, because the more students learn on their own the better. Kaufer advocates moving on to specifics only after it is clear that the student is stuck and cannot respond to more general questions.[8]

When revision needs to move its focus to sentence matters, the length of student sentences is frequently a concern. Some students write strings of short, simple sentences, whereas others create sentences that amble on and on—and on. When the problem is an overreliance on short sentences, students ought to begin by hearing their own sentences as they read their papers aloud. Sentence combining, a heavily researched technique that has become the basis for numerous textbooks, is a useful strategy. But other students are so used to combining and combining that they seem to make only sparing use of periods. Again, a useful technique is to have students read their sentences aloud. The writer of the following sentence would undoubtedly have felt the need to come up for air somewhere in the middle:

> Next you scan the field to the left and see different colors of dirt
> because of the disk, look up the row of darker dirt and you see
> this big cloud of dust because of the disk and you see a green
> tractor with all sorts of heat coming off of it coming down the
> field.

Once students realize the need for breaking up such sentences into more readable units, one strategy is to help them "decombine" by listing all the ideas contained in a typical sentence. The next step is some discussion of which ideas can stay together and which should be separated into new sentences.

When the problem is lack of sentence variety, we need initially to diagnose the cause. Some writers prefer strings of similar sentence patterns marching along because they don't think of making use of all the patterns that sentence combining reminds them they have at their disposal. Other students resist changing sentence patterns for fear of treading into constructions they can't punctuate. Thus, sentence combining is one form of help, while some review of sentence pattern punctuation is a more direct form of help for other students.

At the word level some students need help in locating words used inappropriately. When students can identify words that may need to be revised, however, but can't come up with alternatives, a quick form of help is to ask students to look away from their papers and restate orally what they were trying to say on paper. As they talk and reformulate or explain, they often hear a revision they can use.

For ESL students a different approach is the technique of reformulation. As explained by Andrew Cohen, reformulation is helpful for revising for the kind of fluency and style that make foreign students' prose sound more "native-like."[9] Reformulation begins after an ESL student has had help in correcting all matters of grammar and mechanics, at the stage when the prose is correct, but stylistically still not like that of a native speaker. What the ESL student needs at this stage is for a native English-speaking teacher or tutor to reformulate the paper, that is, to rewrite it by retaining all the student's ideas but in the words of the native speaker. Then, teacher and student carefully compare the differences to help the student see how a native speaker would have said exactly the same thing. The first sentences of the student's and the tutor's reformulated paragraphs from Cohen's example are excerpted here:

> *Non-native speaker of English:* "One of the severe social problems on campus is the problem of the relationship between Arabs and Jews."
>
> *Native speaker's reformulation:* "A serious social problem on the Hebrew University campus is that of relationships between Arabs and Jews."

Eliminating Wordiness

De Beaugrande's *Writing Step by Step*[10] offers students help in editing writing that is, on the other hand, too much influenced by talk. This editing involves the elimination of several types of extra words used in talk:

1. Fillers: words that fill gaps in the stream of talk ("and," "then," "well," "you know," etc.)
2. Hedges: words that soften statements by showing uncertainty or hesitation ("kind of," "sort of," "pretty much," "it seemed to me that," etc.)
3. Repetition: "There are three kinds of X, and of these three kinds of X, . . ."

One way to help students identify these "talk fillers" on the page is to take sample sentences from the student's paper and go over them, asking the student if each word is really needed. To help students decide, we can say the sentence aloud with and then without that word or phrase. Wordiness is best discussed, not in terms of general principles, but with specific examples from students' prose.

And this strategy brings us back to where we began, working with each student and that student's paper. That, of course, requires that we be in the one-to-one setting of student and teacher talking to each other about writing, an excellent setting for the teaching of writing.

The conference is also an excellent setting for helping students with necessary matters of grammar and mechanics. First, though, we need to confront a question that should lead us to a clearer understanding of what the strategies for editing skills offered here are intended to accomplish.

Can Grammar Be Taught?

As teachers of writing, we feel a responsibility to help students master the conventions of standard edited English so that their writing is acceptably correct. Yet, the question of whether grammar can or should be taught has fueled a great deal of research and discussion. Over twenty years ago, in *Research in Written Composition*, Richard Braddock, Richard Lloyd-Jones, and Lowell Schoer emphatically concluded that we ought not to waste our students' time by teaching formal grammar:

> In view of the widespread agreement of research studies based on many types of students and teachers, the conclusion can be stated in strong and unqualified terms: the teaching of formal grammar has a negligible or, because it usually displaces some instruction and practice in actual composition, even a harmful effect on the improvement of writing.[11]

In a more recent assessment of this question, Patrick Hartwell reviews the extensive body of literature that has accumulated on the question of teaching formal grammar and concludes that, for all practical purposes, seventy-five years of experimental research have told us nothing and, furthermore, that more experimental research is not likely to resolve the question.[12] Instead, Hartwell's theory of language predicts little or no value in formal grammar instruction. Hartwell arrives at his conclusion by differentiating among five "grammars," three of which are useful here:

> *Grammar 1:* The grammar in our heads, an internalized and largely unconscious system of rules which allows us to use these rules even when we can't formulate them consciously. For example, while native speakers of English use "the" correctly and will say *the* United States but not *the* England, not everyone can explain the rules being used.
>
> *Grammar 2:* Linguists' descriptions of the language (descriptions which vary from one school of thought to another)
>
> *Grammar 4:* The "rules" of common school grammar (those rules found in grammar texts and handbooks)

As Hartwell demonstrates, Grammar 2, which has no effect on Grammar 1 performance, is of little practical use in the classroom, a conclusion reached earlier in the work of Herbert Seliger. Seliger concluded that "there does not seem to be any discernible correlation between knowing specific rules and performance."[13] As for Grammar 4, its rules are, in the acronym Hartwell borrows from technical writers, COIK—clear only if known. That is, if we already know the rule, the explanation is clear. If, however, we are trying to learn the rule, we won't be able to by reading the rule (a variation on the farmer's retort to the tourist in his area, "You can't get there from here"). Elsewhere Hartwell details reasons for these COIK textbook explanations' failure to teach: "Too often, they offer an inadequate analysis of what might cause a student to make a particular error, and, far too often, they ask the student to behave in ways that are counterproductive to the acquisition of full adult literacy."[14] Robert de Beaugrande is equally critical of the writers of such prose, who offer the reader a choice between what he describes as "the forbiddingly technical and the unworkably vague."[15]

Hartwell's analysis suggests that neither formal instruction in Grammar 2 nor in Grammar 4 leads to control over surface correctness or improvement in the quality of writing. If we agree with such conclusions, we are faced with a seeming dilemma: How then do we help our students? Some teachers would respond that we must encourage the kind of language activities that immerse students in the communicative act so that they can acquire a firmer intuitive knowledge of Grammar 1. Surely, this is part of what teachers can provide; but we may also feel the need to direct attention to specific areas of language use when they plague students' writing. Asking students to read texts, work exercises, or sit through our explanations of rules produces minimal gains at best, as Hartwell's taxonomy of grammars predicts (and as too many of us can confirm from our own experience). But we can, in the one-to-one setting of the conference, move away from formal instruction in grammar and work with a student's own writing. Donald Graves calls this teaching in context, at the point of need.[16] Here, we are no longer merely working on formal grammar, grammar in the abstract, but working with the student on his or her own prose structures.

What Graves calls the "point of need" can be located fairly specifically in the various stages a piece of writing goes through—as revision and editing steps. Integrating help with grammar into the editing stage of writing makes sense for several reasons. If we ask students to attend to misspellings, errors in sentence structure, and so on in first drafts, we may find that for other reasons those corrected words and clauses have disappeared from the next draft. Or we may find that they should disappear but that students, reluctant to discard what they now know is correct, will retain them in the paper no matter how ill-fitting they are. Even more important, encouraging students to attend to such matters in the early stages of a piece of writing also detracts from the student's growing sense of writing as an evolving process, in which draft follows draft and in which the writer's focus should not start out at the word level. What is offered here, however, even at the editing stage, is not merely a reiteration of Grammar 4 rules, but strategies that are tools to work with.

General Strategies for Grammatical Correctness

The conference setting is particularly appropriate for working on grammar as an editing skill because specific errors evident on the page make up the agenda for discussion. Students who don't write fragments don't need to hear what they already know; instead, they can attend to whatever is an evident need in their own writing. Because we can vary our teaching methods in a conference, we can offer help geared to the student's level of understanding and preferred method of learning. But this help can't merely be explanations that are COIK, clear only if known. Instead, we can help students by offering enough of an explanation to start them off and then turning the process of understanding over to them. This can include inviting them to find and revise all instances of whatever problem was discussed, asking questions as they proceed; to reformulate the principle for themselves in terms they are comfortable with; to write their own sentences demonstrating the rule; to cite uses of the rule in their own papers if that seems helpful; or to explain how the rule works in their sentences.

Another approach is to give students patterns to follow in creating their own sentences, patterns that illustrate some rule in operation. Thomas Friedmann suggests a similar approach, the use of non-error-based exercises in which students are offered only correct examples so that they can learn to recognize these correct versions. Friedmann avoids wrong examples because, he argues, they cannot help a student whose sense of what is correct is at best shaky. When students can't spell words correctly because they don't have a correct mental representation of those words, for example, seeing misspellings can merely compound the problem.[17]

Other methods in use have been described in the work of people interested in constructing tutorial programs for computers. What is it, they ask, that human tutors do that computer tutorials should try to imitate? The findings of one study of tutorial dialogues, done by Allan Collins, Eleanor Warnock, and Joseph Passafiuma, are particularly relevant here as suggestions for general conference teaching strategies, even though the subject matter being taught in the study was not writing.[18] What do tutors do? Collins and his colleagues found, first, that tutors build on what the students already know. The teachers examined in this study proceeded by questioning their students to find out the extent of the students' previous knowledge and then taught new material by relating it to that previous knowledge (a strategy particularly helpful in working with grammatical concepts). The study also found that tutors respond directly to student errors. When students made mistakes, tutors questioned them to diagnose the confusion and then provided relevant information to straighten out that confusion. Such tutorials were thus directed against existing confusions rather than toward what the teachers anticipated might be typical student problems, an approach often used in the classroom. Yet another tutorial strategy, identified by Glynda Hull in her work on writing tutorials,[19] involves pointing to places in a paper where there are errors and letting the student identify them. An excerpt from one of Hull's tutorial transcripts, included here, demonstrates this strategy at work. This tutor is particularly adept at helping the student decide where the errors are and assisting in the recall of rules that the student knows but isn't using. When the student isn't sure about one point (whether there's an -*ed* in "used to"), the tutor supplies the needed answer. The result of the session, as the student realizes at the end, is that he's beginning to be a better proofreader of his own writing.

> *Tutor:*   What I want to do here is to tell you the line where there's an error and see if you can find it. So, there's a mistake in the first sentence.

Student: (long pause) Is it a misspelling?

Tutor: Yeah, it is.

Student: (Chuckle.) I guessed it. *Restaurant?* Well, I guess I'd have to look these up. It's between *neighborhood* and *restaurant.*

Tutor: That's wrong. Those are good words to start with. I mean, if I were guessing about which words might be misspelled, I'd choose the long ones. But you've got a word in there with a letter . . .

Student: (interrupting) *First!* I can't believe that. *Fist.* (still chuckling)

Tutor: Okay, now, I want you to look at the sentence, *At night when the light was turn on inside the pig.* There's a mistake in it somewhere.

Student: At night when the light was turn on inside the pig, the mistake is in there somewhere?

Tutor: Yep.

Student: (reading) At night when the light, when the lights, when the light, was turned on inside the pig. It might be that comma . . . ?

Tutor: The comma's okay.

Student: Hmmm. I'm lost.

Tutor: There's something left off a word.

Student: (reading) At night when the light was turn, TURNED! I'm saying it, but I'm not looking! Man, I got to remember that.

Tutor: Good. Come down to the line beginning *My mother use to wash my apron every night and instruct me not to wear it till I got to work.* There's a mistake there.

Student: (reading) It's in the sentence *My mother use to wash?* Put a comma? After night?

Tutor: Check the comma to see what it's joining. You're only going to put a comma when it's joining . . .

Student: Two whole sentences. So it's not the comma. I'm not sure if you put an *ed* after that *use.*

Tutor: You sure do. That's one that's hard to hear. Good.

Student: (nodding and reading) Used to wash.

Tutor: Let's go back up to the sentence, *I worked from 9:00 AM to 5:00 PM on Saturdays and on week days I worked from 4:00 PM to 7:00 PM.* You need a comma there somewhere.

Student: (reading) I worked from 9:00 AM to 5:00 PM on Saturdays, comma.

Tutor: Good. There you've got one sentence joined to another sentence by *and.*

Student: Now I'm beginning to see my own errors. Whenever I see *and, but, so,* or *or,* I can check those.

Yet another general strategy for working on grammatical control of written language at the editing stage involves reading aloud for purposes of proofreading. One form of such proofreading, described by Hartwell in "A Writing Laboratory Model,"[20] involves students' listening to themselves read their papers aloud. In Hartwell's writing lab, students are encouraged to read their papers into a tape recorder and then listen to the playback. As a result, Hartwell reports, they can often identify weaknesses in sentence structure, coherence, and development. Students who leave off -s and -ed endings in writing tend to reinsert them when reading. Rather than dealing with the grammatical concepts involved, such as past tense or regular and irregular verbs, Hartwell offers such students a list of the four spoken realizations of -ed endings that they may be omitting in their writing:

/d/ as in "defined"
/əd/ as in "rounded"
/t/ as in "talked"
/ø/ null realization

When students make this connection, says Hartwell, they can improve surface correctness.

In the writing lab at Northeastern Illinois University, Shelly Samuels uses oral proofreading to diagnose grammar and syntax problems and to provide students with techniques for editing their own writing.[21] Students begin by reading their papers aloud while tutors follow along and note which corrections the students have made verbally. This helps the tutor distinguish among three kinds of errors: (1) those errors the student doesn't notice and doesn't correct orally, (2) those errors the student corrects orally and notes on the page, and (3) those errors the student corrects orally but doesn't see on the page. The advantage of such oral proofreading, notes Samuels, is that it improves students' editing skills and identifies those errors they need to overcome. In contrast, when teachers have only the written products to grade at home, in the traditional mode of teacher response, they do not have a reliable way of deciding in which of the above three categories each written error belongs. Structuring classroom teaching becomes a matter of deciding whether to treat those errors as proofreading problems or as errors due to lack of knowledge.

A variation on Samuels's method of oral proofreading described by Mary King[22] incorporates the strategy noted by Glynda Hull of directing the student's attention to the place in the text where an error occurs, but not identifying the error. King's technique asks the student to read aloud while the teacher notes points at which the student orally corrects but doesn't notice something that is written erroneously. Then, in successive readings, the tutor directs the student's attention not to the error but to the sentence in which the error appears. Initially, the tutor might say, "Read that sentence again," then "Slow down and read it again," and finally, "There is an error in that sentence. Can you find it?" After proceeding through the paper several times in this way, most students, says King, can correct most of their errors. Yet another variation on oral proofreading is Elaine Ware's use of small cards with windows permitting the student to see individual words separated from the text, thus training the student's eye to look at the letters of a word rather than at its meaning.[23]

As these methods indicate, having students read their papers aloud in a conference is a valuable technique. It helps students locate problems on the page and problems that become evident when the paper is heard. For example, the sample of student writing included in appendix B, part 3, as paper 9 is generally so well phrased that the writer, Dan, will undoubtedly hear that the last sentence of the second paragraph needs revision: "This may create a tendency for better reading skills, which would benefit other classes in the respect of the practice of reading it creates and an increased vocabulary." If Dan were asked to read that sentence aloud, he would probably stumble in doing so. Most adequate writers when reading such problem sentences or phrases in their own papers usually launch in and immediately begin revising or considering alternative phrasing. When students read their own writing, they can also hear that they've written sentences that are overly long, that they've omitted punctuation the reader needs, that they've shifted person or tense, or that their writing sounds choppy. Oral proofing is useful for a variety of problems.

Specific Strategies for Grammatical Correctness

The general strategies described above help with a number of grammatical problems, but there are other strategies, such as the ones offered here, designed to assist students with specific difficulties. Since strategies are alternatives to grammatical rules, most do not require an understanding of grammatical terminology. The ones offered here which do make use of terms such as "independent clause" and "dependent clause" are for students who know these terms. For those who do not, such terminology can be acquired by other strategies (also included here) that help students learn concepts such as "subject" and "predicate" and then build on those terms. Some of the strategies described below are used in the writing lab where I teach, and others are typical of the techniques traded at conferences or in journal articles. Still others are borrowed either from Robert de Beaugrande's *Text Production: Toward a Science of Composition* or his book for students, *Writing Step by Step,* a textbook offering students not COIK explanations but strategies for dealing with error that require no expertise in traditional grammar (Hartwell's Grammar 4). De Beaugrande's hypothesis, the basis for his approach, is that the grammar of talk contains all the categories needed for a grammar of writing. These categories can be used by any student who knows how to talk in English. Using everyday speech as their guide, such writers can call upon strategies that help them recognize the most common grammatical problems in writing.

Strategies for Sentence Recognition

In de Beaugrande's approach, students are given two interlocking definitions for sentences: every sentence must have at least one independent clause and every clause must have at least one subject and one predicate. Because students must thus be able to identify independent clauses, subjects, and predicates, they are given strategies to do so.[24]

1. *To find subjects and predicates:* Ask students to make up a "who/what" question about a statement. The predicate of the statement is all the words from the original sentence used in the who/what question, and the subject is the rest:

   The Queen of Hearts made some tarts.

   Who made some tarts?

   (predicate = made some tarts)

   (subject =The Queen of Hearts)

2. *To identify independent clauses:* Ask students to make up a "yes/no" question about the statement in the clause, that is, a question that could be sensibly answered with yes or no. Only independent clauses will yield yes/no questions. (Comma splices will make two yes/no questions.)

   The knave stole some tarts.

   Did the knave steal some tarts? (a sensible question and, therefore, an independent clause)

   Because he was very hungry.

   Because was he very hungry? (not a sensible question and, therefore, not an independent clause)

Such approaches are easily incorporated into conferences and work effectively when the tutor reads over a paper with a student. For those students who do not recognize sentence fragments they have written, using these strategies can help them learn to recognize what the error is.

In addition to de Beaugrande's approach, described above, there are other strategies for helping students recognize fragments:

1. Borrow the linguistic definition of a sentence as an utterance which would be accepted as reasonably complete if made by someone who walked into a room, made the statement, and left. For example, if someone were to walk into a room and say, "It is raining out," most hearers would agree that this is a reasonably complete statement. By contrast, if someone were to walk into a room and say, "Because it is raining out," most hearers would agree that more needs to be said. (Some students grasp the concept fairly quickly; others are perplexed, especially when a pronoun is used as the subject, as in "He is here." They insist that the sentence is incomplete because more needs to be said about who "he" is. As a next step, the teacher can either offer an explanation of pronouns, as described in the next strategy, or move on to another strategy for recognizing fragments.)

2. For students who find visual representations useful, it helps to define a sentence by drawing a quick sketch in the following manner:

   $$\boxed{\text{subj.}} + \boxed{\text{verb}} \ (\text{+ perhaps an object})$$

   Since subjects have either nouns or pronouns, students will need to recognize nouns, which, as de Beaugrande points out, are the words we can put "the" in front of, and pronouns, which can be explained as substitutes for nouns. Verbs, as de Beaugrande points out, are words we can put "didn't" in front of or "not" after. Most verbs take "didn't" (go—didn't go), but helping verbs take "not" (have gone—have not gone). With some practice in finding subjects and verbs, the student can then check any doubtful sentences by looking for the components to fill each box. Students will also need help in distinguishing independent from dependent clauses, for which de Beaugrande's yes/no question is very useful.

3. For students whose sentence fragments are mainly mistakes in punctuation (separating an independent clause from a dependent clause with a period, as in "The picnic was canceled. Because it was raining out"), de Beaugrande's yes/no question or help in recognizing marker words which begin dependent clauses can be

useful. Elsewhere I've described this kind of fragment as constituting a very large percentage of most students' fragments.[25]

4. Proofreading for fragments by reading each sentence from the end of the paper backward to the beginning allows the student to hear each sentence as a separate entity. (A fuller description of this technique can be found in Kathy Martin's "A Quick Check and Cure for Fragments.")[26]

Strategies for Subject-Verb Agreement

It is important here to help students distinguish between those subject-verb errors that occur because of unfamiliarity with appropriate inflectional endings on verbs, those that occur because the student is not sure which word is the verb, and those that occur because so many words have intervened between the subject and the verb that the student's normally reliable aural checking does not work. When students are not sure of all the inflectional endings (that is, whether we say "he walk" or "he walks"), we can offer formulas such as "with third person singular add -s" or have students proofread magazines or newspapers to find verb endings, thereby familiarizing themselves with usage patterns for standard edited English. Another strategy is to have a handout available on the conference table with a list of appropriate verb endings and to ask students to read their papers and check all verb endings to see that their verbs match those patterns on the handout. (Some initial demonstration of this technique may be needed before the student begins. It is a tedious process that some students resist, often because they aren't sufficiently adept at recognizing the verb in a sentence. Stopping to work on verb recognition, as described in the next paragraph, can be useful.)

For those students who are not sure which word is the verb, de Beaugrande's method is helpful for finding the agreeing verb in the predicate. This strategy involves several steps (see *Text Production,* 244, for a fuller description):

1. Insert a "denial word" into a statement (doesn't/don't, didn't/won't).
2. The "agreeing verb" of the original statement is the one located *after* the denial word.
   Example: Our boss wants to call a meeting.
   Our boss doesn't want to call a meeting.
   (This is especially helpful for students who wonder whether "want" or "call" may be the verb here.)

3. If a denial word can't be inserted, try inserting "not" or "-n't."
The agreeing verb is then the one *before* the insertion.
Example: He was given a present.
   He wasn't given a present.
(This is helpful for students who are unsure of whether the
agreeing verb is "was" or "given."

Another technique for students who need help in locating verbs is
to ask them to find the word which changes when the sentence is
switched from past to present tense or present to past tense. (Like
many other strategies, this too is not universally applicable. In this
case the strategy is limited by the exceptions it does not account for,
verbs such as "put" and "set" which do not change form.)

For students who make subject-verb agreement errors because of
intervening words (e.g., "The committee selected to deal with all those
problems ask for an extension for the report"), proofreading the paper
to locate subjects and verbs is a helpful approach. Reading sentence
by sentence from the end of the paper to the beginning can also help
the reader look at each sentence and not the general flow of meaning.

Strategies for Comma Errors

The most frequent student errors in comma usage are comma splices
and run-ons (which can be dealt with by de Beaugrande's method of
identifying independent clauses with yes/no questions) and missing
commas after introductory clauses, with nonessential (or nonrestric-
tive) clauses and phrases, and with coordinating adjectives. For those
students who can hear pauses and intonation curves in their voices,
these oral markers can be used to help identify visual markers needed
on the page. Although many students can mislead themselves into
using inappropriate pause markers as well, suggesting the use of reading aloud to note places where punctuation is needed can be helpful
for some. This is especially helpful when students frequently omit the
comma after a long introductory clause but can hear the need for a
breath pause at the appropriate place.

For visually oriented students and/or for those who like formulas,
a visual pattern sheet can be useful. In our writing lab, one of the
handouts offers a visual chart, similar to the one illustrated here,
which for some students not only shows how they can manipulate
options but also indicates that punctuation rules are not a vast reser-
voir of complex mysteries but a limited set of ways to mark sentences.

Punctuation Pattern Sheet

1. | Independent clause | .

2. | Independent clause | ; | independent clause | .

3. | Independent clause | ;   therefore, | independent clause | .
                     however,
                     nevertheless,
                     consequently,
                     furthermore,
                     moreover,
                         (etc.)

4. | Independent clause | ,   and | independent clause | .
                     but
                     for
                     or
                     nor
                     so
                     yet

5. | Clause, phrase, or word | nonessential clause, , phrase, or word, | clause, phrase, or word | .

6. If | dependent clause | , | independent clause | .
Because
Since
When
While
Although
After
    (etc.)

7. | Independent clause | if | dependent clause | .
                     because
                     since
                     when
                     while
                     although
                     after
                       (etc.)

8. | Independent clause | :   A, B, and C.

9. "_____," she said.

   He said, "_____."

   "_____," she said, "_____."

A somewhat different representation (less visual, more formulaic) of comma and semicolon options has been developed by Robert Child for students who can identify clauses:

Correct patterns	Some possible wrong patterns
IC. IC.	IC, IC.
IC; IC.	IC IC.
IC; IM, IC. (or) IC. IM, IC.	
IC, CC IC.	
IC DM DC.	IC, DM DC.
DM DC, IC.	DM DC IC.

Key to abbreviations:
IC = independent clause
IM = independent marker (therefore, moreover, thus, etc.)
DM = dependent marker (because, if, as, when, while, etc.)
DC = dependent clause
CC = coordinating conjunction (and, but, for, or, nor, so, yet)

For students having trouble with inserting commas correctly in a series of modifiers, de Beaugrande (in *Writing Step by Step*, 340–41) recommends seeing if the modifiers can be moved around. If so, then a comma is needed.

> *Example:* peaceful, undisturbed life
>
> > undisturbed, peaceful life (a comma can therefore be inserted)
>
> > small silver platter
> > *not* silver small platter (a comma therefore cannot be inserted)

Strategies for Spelling

The first step in working on spelling errors is separating those errors caused by overload or inattention (which can be corrected with proofreading strategies such as those described above) from those caused by ignorance of the correct spelling. In addition, I have argued elsewhere (in "Visualization and Spelling Competence") that because visualization is very important in spelling competence, it is helpful to offer students strategies designed to improve their ability to focus attention on those letters in words which they have not noticed and therefore have not stored correctly in memory. One way to do this is to contrast for the student the errors in the misspelled word with the correct letters in the word. For example, if the student has written the word "collage" instead of "college," it is helpful first to write the word as the student spelled it originally, then to write the correctly spelled word and to call attention to the letter "e." Categorizing types of errors is another strategy which helps students find clusters of errors, some of which may be due to a consistent principle at work, such as the following:

1. doubled consonants (totaly vs. totally)
2. missing letters in syllables (convience vs. convenience)
3. homophones (their/there/they're; your/you're; it's/its)

Further discussion of helping students categorize errors can be found in Mina Shaughnessy's *Errors and Expectations* and Chopeta Lyons's "Spelling Inventories."[27] Other strategies for working on spelling include help with syllabication[28] and the use of the tactile kinesthetic method, in which students trace words with their fingers several times, saying the word aloud as they proceed.[29]

Strategies for Other Grammatical Errors

While a large portion of student errors falls into the categories listed above, there are other, less frequent, but persistent errors that crop up in some students' papers and may need some attention. Pronoun problems in which the pronoun does not agree with its referent can be overcome by working with students at the proofing stage as they circle pronouns and find the word each pronoun refers to. Once this is done, most students can see that "it" does not equal or take the place of "the books." Vague pronoun reference can be worked on in terms of the audience confusion it causes. That is, as the teacher and student read through the paper, the teacher can demonstrate by asking for clarification of what a vague "it" or "they" means. Or teachers can let themselves react as readers and tell the writer the possible alternatives that occur to them. For example, in paper 11 in appendix B, Michael's prose moves along clearly until the third paragraph, where he writes: "Now I don't know about you, but this also is one of my most hated things." The reader here can simply ask if "this" refers to taking out garbage or having to do it in the middle of his favorite TV show.

After a few rounds of this, most students eventually begin to anticipate reader problems with their pronouns.

Consistency of verb tense or person can also be checked by having students read their papers and asking, "Is that sentence in present or past tense?" Inconsistencies become very noticeable this way as the student and teacher proceed through a paragraph or a page. Lack of parallel structure also becomes apparent if attention is called to the dissimilar sounds of elements in a string of similar words or phrases. Robert Child, in his dissertation work in progress on teacher-induced student error, has noted that some faulty parallelism is due to students' attempts to avoid redundancy, a stylistic problem teachers have emphasized. For example, the sentence "I wanted to hear what questions he asked and his answers to the moderator" may be a student's attempt to avoid the repetition involved in keeping parallel form in a more appropriate version, "I wanted to hear what questions he asked and what his answers to the moderator were."

Dangling modifiers, another common error, are difficult for some students to spot, especially when they have constructed dangling modifiers in an attempt to follow a teacher's injunction to avoid "I." "Walking down the street, a truck was seen" can be a student's attempt to keep first person out of his or her paper. We can help students recognize such a construction when, as they read the initial phrase, we ask who will perform the action. For example, when a student has written "Waiting for my friend to call, the TV helped to pass the time," we can call a halt after "Waiting for my friend to call" and explain that we as readers don't know who is waiting, but that we'll find out when we come to the subject of the main clause. Most students can quickly see that the TV was not waiting.

Conclusion

The strategies described in this chapter do not resemble the usual textbook explanations that state rules and give examples or offer a list of guidelines to follow that are then illustrated in sample paragraphs and essays. Instead, in the conference, teacher and student are working together on the student's own writing, thereby attending to the particular needs of that student and acknowledging his or her uniqueness. When the teacher helps the student focus on learning something, it is more likely to be a strategy to use in the process of drafting and redrafting the paper. The difference, a crucial one, is that the need is real and immediate. The problem area under consideration is not some generalization in a textbook but is there on the page in front of the writer. In addition, students apply strategies directly to their own writing rather than having to figure out how and where a rule applies.

Selecting strategies to use may seem like a complicated process, having been the topic of discussion for several chapters of this book. To the new teacher or tutor, the first impression may be that there is too much to attend to simultaneously in a tutorial. Initially overwhelmed, such a newcomer may freeze, not knowing what to do first, and need to be reminded that, when in doubt, the most important thing is to keep in mind one question: How can I help this student sitting next to me become a better writer? It is also helpful to remember that there is no right conference, no one path along which it should progress. Conference conversations can take a seemingly infinite variety of twists and turns. That conferences are not mysterious but very normal conversations can be seen by reading the excerpts at the back of this book, people talking with people. Some of the teachers involved in those conversations are more skilled; others are learning. Fortunately, students are as forgiving of us as we learn as we should be of them as they learn. And the conference is a superb setting for all of this learning to take place.

Notes

1. See, for example, the questionnaire in my *Practice for a Purpose* (Boston: Houghton Mifflin, 1984).

2. Linda Flower and John R. Hayes, "Problem-Solving Strategies and the Writing Process," *College English* 39 (1977): 449–61.

3. Robert Child, dissertation in progress, Purdue University.

4. Peter Elbow, "The Doubting Game and the Believing Game: Summary of Work in Progress and Request for Help," *PRE/TEXT* 3 (1982): 339–51.

5. Peter Schiff, *The Teacher-Student Writing Conference: New Approaches* (Urbana, Ill.: ERIC Clearinghouse on Reading and Communication Skills, 1978), ED 165 190.

6. James C. Collins, "Dialogue and Monologue and the Unskilled Writer," *English Journal* 71 (Apr. 1982): 84–86.

7. Walker Gibson, "The Writing Teacher as a Dumb Reader," *College Composition and Communication* 30 (1979): 192.

8. David Kaufer, "An Intelligent Tutor for Teaching Revision" (Paper delivered at the Conference on College Composition and Communication, Minneapolis, 21 March 1985).

9. See Andrew Cohen, "Reformulation: Another Way to Get Feedback," *Writing Lab Newsletter* 10, no. 2 (1985): 6–10.

10. Robert de Beaugrande, *Writing Step by Step* (San Diego: Harcourt Brace Jovanovich, 1985).

11. Richard Braddock, Richard Lloyd-Jones, and Lowell Schoer, *Research in Written Composition* (Champaign, Ill.: National Council of Teachers of English, 1963).

12. Patrick Hartwell, "Grammar, Grammars, and the Teaching of Grammar," *College English* 47 (1985): 105–27.

13. Herbert W. Seliger, "On the Nature and Function of Language Roles in Language Teaching," *TESOL Quarterly* 13 (1979): 359–69.

14. Patrick Hartwell, "Paradoxes and Problems: The Value of Traditional Textbook Rules," *Pennsylvania Writing Project Newsletter* 3, no. 2–3 (1983): 9.

15. Robert de Beaugrande, *Text Production: Toward a Science of Composition* (Norwood, N.J.: Ablex, 1984).

16. Quoted in Jan Turbill, *No Better Way to Teach Writing* (Rosebery, N.S.W., Australia: Primary English Teaching Association, 1982).

17. Thomas Friedmann, "A Blueprint for Writing Lab Exercises," *Writing Lab Newsletter* 8, no. 5 (1984): 1–4.

18. Allan Collins, Eleanor H. Warnock, and Joseph J. Passafiuma, "Analysis and Synthesis of Tutorial Dialogues," in vol. 9 of *The Psychology of Learning and Motivation*, ed. Gordon H. Bowes (New York: Academic Press, 1975), 49–87.

19. Glynda Hull, "Using Computers to Study Error and to Teach Editing: An Interim Project Report" (Paper delivered at the Conference on College Composition and Communication, Minneapolis, 22 March 1985).

20. Patrick Hartwell, "A Writing Laboratory Model," in *Basic Writing*, ed. Lawrence N. Kasden and Daniel R. Hoeber (Urbana, Ill.: National Council of Teachers of English, 1980), 69.

21. Shelly Samuels, "Emphasizing Oral Proofreading in the Writing Lab: A Multifunction Technique for Both Tutors and Students," *Writing Lab Newsletter* 9, no. 2 (1984): 1–4.

22. Mary King, "Proofreading Is Not Reading," *Teaching English in the Two-Year College* 12 (1985): 108–12.

23. Elaine Ware, "Visual Perception through 'Window Proofreading,'" *Writing Lab Newsletter* 9, no. 9 (1985): 8–9.

24. The following strategies are from Robert de Beaugrande, "Forward to the Basics: Getting Down to Grammar," *College Composition and Communication* 35 (1984): 362–67 and *Text Production*, 240–42.

25. Muriel Harris, "Mending the Fragmented Free Modifier," *College Composition and Communication* 28 (1981): 175–82.

26. Kathy Martin, "A Quick Check and Cure for Fragments," *Writing Lab Newsletter* 8, no. 7 (1984): 4.

27. Mina P. Shaughnessy, *Errors and Expectations* (New York: Oxford Univ. Press, 1977); and Chopeta Lyons, "Spelling Inventories," *Writing Lab Newsletter* 6, no. 4 (1982): 2–3.

28. Julie Along and Beverly Lyon Clark, "A Tutor Tutors Spelling," *Writing Lab Newsletter* 6, no. 4 (1981): 3–4.

29. Janice Kleen, "The Teaching of Spelling: A Success Story," *Writing Lab Newsletter* 6, no. 4 (1981): 1–2.

Bibliography

Along, Julie, and Beverly Lyon Clark. "A Tutor Tutors Spelling." *Writing Lab Newsletter* 6, no. 4 (1981): 3–4.

Arbur, Rosemary. "The Student-Teacher Conference." *College Composition and Communication* 28 (1977): 338–42.

Bamberg, Betty. "The Writing Lab and the Composition Class: A Fruitful Collaboration." In *Tutoring Writing: A Sourcebook for Writing Labs*, edited by Muriel Harris, 179–85. Glenview, Ill.: Scott, Foresman, 1982.

Bartholomae, David. "The Study of Error." *College Composition and Communication* 31 (1980): 253–69.

Blenski, Michael, Jr. "The Conference Evaluation: A Renewal." In *They Really Taught Us How to Write*, edited by Patricia Geuder, Linda Harvey, Dennis Loyd, and Jack Wages, 136–40. Urbana, Ill.: National Council of Teachers of English, 1974.

Blonston, Gary. "The Translator." *Science 85* 6, no. 6 (1985): 78–85.

Braddock, Richard, Richard Lloyd-Jones, and Lowell Schoer. *Research in Written Composition*. Champaign, Ill.: National Council of Teachers of English, 1963.

Brostoff, Anita. "The Writing Conference: Foundations." In *Tutoring Writing: A Sourcebook for Writing Labs*, edited by Muriel Harris, 21–26. Glenview, Ill.: Scott, Foresman, 1982.

Bruner, Jerome. *Toward a Theory of Instruction*. Cambridge, Mass.: Belknap Press, 1967.

Budz, Judith, and Terry Grabar. "Tutorial versus Classroom in Freshman English." *College English* 37 (1976): 654–56.

Canuteson, John. *Conferences as Evaluation Devices in Freshman Composition*. Urbana, Ill.: ERIC Clearinghouse on Reading and Communication Skills, 1977. ED 143 027.

Carnicelli, Thomas A. "The Writing Conference: A One-to-One Conversation." In *Eight Approaches to Teaching Composition*, edited by Timothy Donovan and Ben McClelland, 101–31. Urbana, Ill.: National Council of Teachers of English, 1980.

Cohen, Andrew. "Reformulation: Another Way to Get Feedback." *Writing Lab Newsletter* 10, no. 2 (1985): 6–10.

———. "Student Processing of Feedback on Their Compositions." In *Learner Strategies: Research Directions and Educational Implications*, edited by A. Wenden and J. Rubin. London: Pergamon, forthcoming.

Collins, Allan, Eleanor H. Warnock, and Joseph J. Passafiuma. "Analysis and Synthesis of Tutorial Dialogues." In *The Psychology of Learning and Motivation*, edited by Gordon H. Bowes, 9:49–87. New York: Academic Press, 1975.

Collins, James C. "Dialogue and Monologue and the Unskilled Writer." *English Journal* 71 (Apr. 1982): 84–86.

Collins, James C., and Charles Moran. "The Secondary-Level Writing Laboratory: A Report from the Field." In *Tutoring Writing: A Sourcebook for Writing Labs,* edited by Muriel Harris, 196–204. Glenview, Ill.: Scott, Foresman, 1982.

Cooper, Charles. "Responding to Student Writing." In *The Writing Processes of Students,* edited by W. Petty and P. J. Price. Buffalo: Department of Curriculum and Instruction, State University of New York at Buffalo, 1975.

———. "Teaching Writing by Conferencing." In *Survival through Language: The Basics and Beyond,* edited by Rita Bean, Allen Berger, and Anthony Petrosky, 7–22. Pittsburgh, Pa.: School of Education, Pittsburgh Univ., 1977.

Daiute, Colette. "Psycholinguistic Foundations of the Writing Process." *Research in the Teaching of English* 15 (1981): 5–22.

Daly, John A. "Writing Apprehension." In *When a Writer Can't Write,* edited by Mike Rose, 43–82. New York: Guilford, 1985.

Daly, John A., and Miller, M. "The Empirical Development of an Instrument to Measure Writing Apprehension." *Research in the Teaching of English* 9 (1975): 242–49.

Dawe, Charles, and Edward Dornan. Instructor's manual for *One-to-One: Resources for Conference-Centered Writing.* 2d ed. Boston: Little, Brown, 1984.

de Beaugrande, Robert. "Forward to the Basics: Getting Down to Grammar." *College Composition and Communication* 35 (1984): 358–67.

———. *Text Production: Toward a Science of Composition.* Norwood, N.J.: Ablex, 1984.

———. *Writing Step by Step.* San Diego: Harcourt Brace Jovanovich, 1985.

Duke, Charles R. "The Student-Centered Conference and the Writing Process." *English Journal* 64 (1975): 44–47.

Elbow, Peter. "The Doubting Game and the Believing Game: Summary of Work in Progress and Request for Help." *PRE/TEXT* 3 (1982): 339–51.

Ellis, Andrew W. *Reading, Writing, and Dyslexia: A Cognitive Analysis.* Hillsdale, N.J.: Lawrence Erlbaum Associates, 1984.

Emig, Janet. "We Are Trying Conferences." *English Journal* 49 (1960): 223–28.

Ewald, Helen Rothschild. "Using Error Analysis in the Writing Lab for Correctness and Effectiveness." *Writing Lab Newsletter* 8, no. 5 (1984): 6–8.

Farmer, W. L. *Individualized Evaluation as a Method of Instruction to Improve Writing Ability in Freshman College Composition.* Urbana, Ill.: ERIC Clearinghouse on Reading and Communication Skills, 1976. ED 133 759.

Fassler, Barbara. "The Red Pen Revisited: Teaching Composition through Student Conferences." *College Composition and Communication* 40 (1978): 186–90.

Fisher, Lester A., and Donald Murray. "Perhaps the Professor Should Cut Class." *College English* 35 (1973): 169–73.

Flower, Linda, and John R. Hayes. "Problem-Solving Strategies and the Writing Process." *College English* 39 (1977): 449–61.

Freedman, Sarah W. "Evaluation in the Writing Conference: An Interactive Process." In *Selected Papers from the 1981 Texas Writing Research Conference*, edited by Maxine Hairston and Cynthia Selfe, 65–96. Austin: Univ. of Texas at Austin Press, 1981.

———. *Teaching and Learning in the Writing Conference*. Urbana, Ill.: ERIC Clearinghouse on Reading and Communication Skills, 1980. ED 185 599.

Freedman, Sarah W., et al. *The Role of Response in the Acquisition of Written Language*. Final Report to the National Institute of Education, 1985. NIE-G-083-0065. ED 260 407.

Freedman, Sarah W., and Anne Marie Katz. "Pedagogical Interaction during the Composing Process: The Writing Conference." In *Writing in Real Time: Modeling Production Processes*, edited by Ann Matsuhashi. Norwood, N.J.: Ablex, forthcoming.

Freedman, Sarah W., and Ellen Nold. "On Budz and Grabar's 'Tutorial vs. Classroom' Study." *College English* 38 (1976): 427–29.

Freedman, Sarah W., and Melanie Sperling. "Written Language Acquisition: The Role of Response and the Writing Conference." In *The Acquisition of Written Language: Response and Revision*, edited by Sarah W. Freedman. Norwood, N.J.: Ablex, 1985.

Freeman, Donald C. "Linguistics and Error Analysis: On Agency." *Linguistics, Stylistics, and the Teaching of Composition*, edited by Donald McQuade, 143–50. Akron, Ohio: Dept. of English, Univ. of Akron, 1979.

Friedmann, Thomas. "A Blueprint for Writing Lab Exercises." *Writing Lab Newsletter* 8, no. 5 (1984): 1–4.

Fritts, Mildred F. "The Effects of Individual Teacher Conferences on the Writing Achievement and Self-Concept of Developmental Junior College Writing Students." *DAI* 37 (1977): 4185A. ED 138 988.

Garrison, Roger. "One-to-One: Tutorial Instruction in Freshman Composition." *New Directions for Community Colleges* 2 (1974): 55–84.

Gates, Allan F. "A Study of the Effects of Work Undertaken in an Independent Learning Center by Marginal Students at Marshalltown Community College." *DAI* 37 (1977): 7002A.

Gibson, Walker. "The Writing Teacher as a Dumb Reader." *College Composition and Communication* 30 (1979): 192–95.

Gills, Paula. "A Reader Responds." *Writing Lab Newsletter* 9, no. 8 (1985): 6–8.

Graves, Donald. "Let's Get Rid of the Welfare Mess in the Teaching of Children." *Language Arts* 53 (1976): 645–51.

———. *Writing: Teachers and Children at Work*. Portsmouth, N.H.: Heinemann, 1983.

Gutschow, Deanna. "Stopping the March through Georgia." In *On Righting Writing: Classroom Practices in Teaching English 1975–76*, edited by Ouida Clapp, 96–100. Urbana, Ill.: National Council of Teachers of English, 1975.

Hall, Edward T. *Beyond Culture*. Garden City, N.Y.: Doubleday, Anchor Press, 1977.

――. *The Hidden Dimension.* Garden City, N.Y.: Doubleday, Anchor Press, 1969.

――. *The Silent Language.* New York: Doubleday, 1959.

Harris, Muriel. "Contradictory Perceptions of Rules for Writing." *College Composition and Communication* 30 (1979): 218-20.

――. "Diagnosing Writing Process Problems: A Pedagogical Application of Speaking-Aloud Protocol Analyses." In *When a Writer Can't Write: Research in Writer's Block and Other Writing Process Problems,* edited by Mike Rose, 166-81. New York: Guilford, 1985.

――. "Individualized Diagnosis: Searching for Causes, Not Symptoms of Writing Deficiencies." *College English* 40 (1978): 64-69.

――. "Mending the Fragmented Free Modifier." *College Composition and Communication* 28 (1981): 175-82.

――. "Modeling: A Process Method of Teaching." *College English* 45 (1983): 74-84.

――. "The Overgraded Paper: Another Case of More Is Less." In *How to Handle the Paper Load: Classroom Practices in Teaching English 1979-80,* edited by Gene Stanford, 91-94. Urbana, Ill.: National Council of Teachers of English, 1979.

――. *Practice for a Purpose.* Boston: Houghton Mifflin, 1984.

――. "The Roles a Tutor Plays." *English Journal* 69 (1980): 62-65.

――. "Visualization and Spelling Competence." *Journal of Remedial and Developmental Education* 9, no. 2 (1985): 2-5.

――, ed. *1984 Writing Lab Directory.* West Lafayette, Ind.: Dept. of English, Purdue Univ., 1984.

Harris, Winifred H. "Teacher Response to Student Writing: A Study of the Response Patterns of High School English Teachers to Determine the Bases for Teacher Judgment of Student Writing." *Research in the Teaching of English* 11 (1977): 175-85.

Hartwell, Patrick. "Grammar, Grammars, and the Teaching of Grammar." *College English* 47 (1985): 105-27.

――. "Paradoxes and Problems: The Value of Traditional Textbook Rules." *Pennsylvania Writing Project Newsletter* 3, no. 2-3 (1983): 7-10.

――. "A Writing Laboratory Model." In *Basic Writing,* edited by Lawrence N. Kasden and Daniel R. Hoeber, 63-73. Urbana, Ill.: National Council of Teachers of English, 1980.

Hawes, Lorna, and Barbara Richards. *A Workshop Approach to Teaching Composition.* Urbana, Ill.: ERIC Clearinghouse on Reading and Communication Skills, 1977. ED 155 936.

Hawkins, Thom. "Intimacy and Audience: The Relation between Revision and the Social Dimension of Peer Tutoring." *College English* 42 (1980): 64-68.

Hayes, Mary F., and Donald Daiker. "Using Protocol Analysis in Evaluating Responses to Student Writing." *Freshman English News* 13, no. 2 (1984): 1-4.

Hiatt, Mary. "Students at Bay: The Myth of the Conference." *College Composition and Communication* 26 (1975): 38-41.

Hinds, John. "Reader versus Writer Responsibility: A New Typology." In *Analyzing Writing: Models and Methods,* edited by Ulla Connor and Robert B. Kaplan. Reading, Mass.: Addison-Wesley, forthcoming.

Holbrook, Hilary Taylor. "ERIC/RCS Report: Whither (Wither) Grammar?" *Language Arts* 60 (1983): 259–63.

Hull, Glynda. "Using Computers to Study Error and to Teach Editing: An Interim Project Report." Paper presented at the annual meeting of the Conference on College Composition and Communication, Minneapolis, 22 March 1985.

Irmscher, William F. Review of *The Writer's Mind: Writing as a Mode of Thinking,* edited by Janice N. Hays, Phyllis A. Roth, Jon R. Ramsey, and Robert D. Foulke. *College Composition and Communication* 35 (1983): 368–69.

Jacobs, Suzanne E., and Adela B. Karliner. "Helping Writers to Think: The Effects of Speech Roles in Individual Conferences on the Quality of Thought in Student Writing." *College English* 38 (1977): 489–505.

Jacoby, Jay. "Shall We Talk to Them in 'English'? The Contributions of Sociolinguistics to Training Writing Center Personnel." In *Proceedings of the Writing Centers Association Fifth Annual Conference,* edited by Muriel Harris and Tracey Baker, 108–32. West Lafayette, Ind.: Dept. of English, Purdue University, 1983.

———. "Training Writing Center Personnel to Work with International Students: The Least We Need to Know." *Writing Lab Newsletter* 10, no. 2 (1985): 1–6.

Jensen, George H., and John K. DiTiberio. "Personality and Individual Writing Processes." *College Composition and Communication* 35 (1984): 285–300.

Johnson, JoAnn B. "Reevaluation of the Question as a Teaching Tool." *Writing Lab Newsletter* 10, no. 4 (1985): 1–4.

Kaplan, Robert B. "Cultural Thought Patterns in Inter-Cultural Education." *Language Learning* 16 (1966): 1–20.

———. "Cultural Thought Patterns Revisited." In *Analyzing Writing: Models and Methods,* edited by Ulla Connor and Robert B. Kaplan. Reading, Mass.: Addison-Wesley, forthcoming.

Kates, Jack. *Individual Conferences versus Typed Comments without Conferences on Graded Freshman English Composition Papers: The El Camino Experiment and the Compton Experiment.* Urbana, Ill.: ERIC Clearinghouse on Reading and Communication Skills, 1977. ED 140 910.

Kaufer, David. "An Intelligent Tutor for Teaching Revision." Paper presented at the annual meeting of the Conference on College Composition and Communication, Minneapolis, 21 March 1985.

King, Mary. "Proofreading Is Not Reading." *Teaching English in the Two-Year College* 12 (1985): 108–12.

Kinkead, Joyce. "Tutors in the Writing Center." Paper presented at the annual meeting of the Conference on College Composition and Communication, Minneapolis, 22 March 1985.

Kirby, Dan, and Tom Liner. *Inside Out: Developmental Strategies for Teaching Writing.* Upper Montclair, N.J.: Boynton/Cook, 1981.

Kleen, Janice. "The Teaching of Spelling: A Success Story." *Writing Lab Newsletter* 6, no. 4 (1981): 1–2.

Knapp, John V. "Contract/Conference Evaluations of Freshman Composition." *College English* 37 (1976): 647–53.

Kollman, Judith. "How to Teach Composition on an Individual Basis—and Survive." *Journal of English Teaching Techniques* 8 (Summer 1975): 13–17.

Kroll, Barry. "Some Developmental Principles for Teaching Composition." In *Rhetoric and Composition*, rev. ed., edited by Richard Graves, 258–62. Upper Montclair, N.J.: Boynton/Cook, 1984.

Lauby, Jacqueline. "Understanding the Dyslexic Writer." *Writing Lab Newsletter* 9, no. 5 (1985): 7–9.

Leeson, Lee Ann. "All of the Answers or Some of the Questions? Teacher as Learner in the Writing Center." *Writing Center Journal* 2, no. 2 (1982): 18–23.

LeTourneau, Mark. "Typical ESL Errors and Tutoring Strategies." *Writing Lab Newsletter* 9, no. 7 (1985): 5–8.

Luban, Nina, Ann Matsuhashi, and Tom Reigstad. "One-to-One to Write: Establishing an Individual-Conference Writing Place." *English Journal* 67 (Nov. 1978): 30–35.

Lyons, Chopeta. "Spelling Inventories." *Writing Lab Newsletter* 6, no. 4 (1982): 2–3.

McCallister, Lois. "Tell Me What You Had in Mind." *English Journal* 59 (1970): 231–34.

MacLeish, Archibald. "On the Teaching of Writing." *Harper's*, Oct. 1959, 158–61.

Madigan, Chris. "A Coding Scheme for Analyzing Student-Teacher Writing Conferences." Paper presented at the annual meeting of the Conference on College Composition and Communication, Minneapolis, 22 March 1985.

Martin, Kathy. "A Quick Check and Cure for Fragments." *Writing Lab Newsletter* 8, no. 7 (1984): 4.

Matalene, Carolyn. "Contrastive Rhetoric: An American Writing Teacher in China." *College English* 47 (1985): 789–808.

Memering, W. Dean. "Talking to Students: Group Conferences." *College Composition and Communication* 24 (1973): 306–7.

Mills, Helen. "Diagnosing Writing Problems and Identifying Learning Disabilities in the Writing Lab." In *Tutoring Writing: A Sourcebook for Writing Labs*, edited by Muriel Harris, 74–83. Glenview, Ill.: Scott, Foresman, 1982.

Moffett, James. "Writing, Inner Speech, and Meditation." In *Rhetoric and Composition*, rev. ed., edited by Richard Graves, 65–80. Upper Montclair, N.J.: Boynton/Cook, 1984.

Murray, Donald. "The Listening Eye: Reflections on the Writing Conference." *College English* 41 (1979): 13–18.

———. "Teaching the Other Self." *College Composition and Communication* 33 (1982): 140–47.

———. *A Writer Teaches Writing: A Practical Method of Teaching Composition*. Boston: Houghton Mifflin, 1968.

Neuleib, Janice. "The Relation of Formal Grammar to Composition." *College Composition and Communication* 28 (1977): 247–50.

Newkirk, Thomas. "Directions and Misdirections in Peer Response." *College Composition and Communication* 35 (1984): 301–11.

North, Stephen. "The Idea of a Writing Center." *College English* 46 (1984): 433–46.

————. "Writing Center Diagnosis: The Composing Profile." In *Tutoring Writing: A Sourcebook for Writing Labs,* edited by Muriel Harris, 42–52. Glenview, Ill.: Scott, Foresman, 1982.

Pask, G., and B.C.E. Scott. "Learning Strategies and Individual Competence." *International Journal of Man-Machine Studies* 4 (1972): 217–53.

Reigstad, Thomas J. "The Writing Conference: An Ethnographic Model for Discovering Patterns of Teacher-Student Interaction." *Writing Center Journal* 2, no. 1 (1982): 9–20.

Reigstad, Thomas J., and Donald A. McAndrew. *Training Tutors for Writing Conferences.* Urbana, Ill.: ERIC Clearinghouse on Reading and Communication Skills and National Council of Teachers of English, 1984.

Rose, Alan. "Spoken versus Written Criticism of Student Writing: Some Advantages of the Conference Method." *College Composition and Communication* 33 (1982): 326–31.

Rose, Mike. "Rigid Rules, Inflexible Plans, and the Stifling of Language: A Cognitivist Analysis of Writer's Block." *College Composition and Communication* 31 (1980): 389–401.

————. *Writer's Block: The Cognitive Dimension.* Carbondale, Ill.: Southern Illinois Univ. Press, 1984.

Ross, Donald. *Individual Writing Conferences: An Approach to Advanced Composition and Technical Writing.* Urbana, Ill.: ERIC Clearinghouse on Reading and Communication Skills, 1973. ED 090 537.

Samuels, Shelly. "Emphasizing Oral Proofreading in the Writing Lab: A Multifunction Technique for Both Tutors and Students." *Writing Lab Newsletter* 9, no. 2 (1984): 1–4.

Scanlon, Leone. "Learning Disabled Students at the Writing Center." *Writing Lab Newsletter* 9, no. 5 (1985): 9–11.

Schiff, Peter. *The Teacher-Student Writing Conference: New Approaches.* Urbana, Ill.: ERIC Clearinghouse on Reading and Communication Skills, 1978. ED 165 190.

Seckendorf, Meg Hess. "The Dynamics of a Student-Tutor Conference: A Case Study." Paper presented at the annual meeting of the Conference on College Composition and Communication, Minneapolis, 22 March 1985.

Selfe, Cynthia L. "An Apprehensive Writer Composes." *When a Writer Can't Write,* edited by Mike Rose, 83–95. New York: Guilford, 1985.

Seliger, Herbert W. "On the Nature and Function of Language Roles in Language Teaching." *TESOL Quarterly* 13 (1979): 359–69.

Selzer, Jack. "Exploring Options in Composing." *College Composition and Communication* 35 (1984): 276–84.

Shaughnessy, Mina P. *Errors and Expectations: A Guide for the Teacher of Basic Writing.* New York: Oxford Univ. Press, 1977.

Shaver, J. P., and D. Nuhn. "The Effectiveness of Tutoring Underachievers in Reading and Writing." *The Journal of Educational Research* 65, no. 3 (1971): 107–12.

Simmons, Jo An McGuire. "The One-to-One Method of Teaching Composition." *College Composition and Communication* 35 (1984): 222–29.

Smith, Myrna, and Barbara Bretcko. "Research on Individual Composition Conferences." Urbana, Ill.: ERIC Clearinghouse on Reading and Communication Skills, 1974. ED 091 709.

Sommers, Nancy. "Responding to Student Writing." *College Composition and Communication* 33 (1982): 148–56.

Sorenson, Sharon. "The High-School Writing Lab: Its Feasibility and Function." In *Tutoring Writing: A Sourcebook for Writing Labs,* edited by Muriel Harris, 186–95. Glenview, Ill.: Scott, Foresman, 1982.

Squire, James R., and Roger K. Applebee. *High School English Instruction Today: The National Study of High School English Programs.* New York: Appleton-Century-Crofts, 1968.

Steward, Joyce, and Mary Croft. *The Writing Laboratory.* Glenview, Ill.: Scott, Foresman, 1982.

Sullivan, F. J., and Donald C. Freeman. "The Interaction of Agency and Affect in Diagnosing and Remedying Syntactic Errors." Temple University Working Papers in Composition. Philadelphia: Dept. of English, Temple Univ., n.d.

Sutton, D. G., and D. S. Arnold. "The Effects of Two Methods of Compensatory Freshman English." *Research in the Teaching of English* 8 (1974): 241–49.

Taylor, David. "A Counseling Approach to Writing Conferences." Paper presented at the Writing Centers Association East Central Conference, Erie, Pennsylvania, 4 May 1985.

———. "Beyond Howdy Doody." *Writing Lab Newsletter,* forthcoming.

———. "Identifying and Helping the Dyslexic Writer." *Journal of Developmental Education* 9, no. 2 (1985): 8–11.

Thompson-Panos, Karyn, and Maria Thomas-Ruzic. "The Least You Should Know about Arabic: Implications for the ESL Writing Instructor." *TESOL Quarterly* 17 (1983): 609–23.

Turbill, Jan. *No Better Way to Teach Writing.* Rosebery, N.S.W., Australia: Primary English Teaching Association, 1982.

Ware, Elaine. "Visual Perception through 'Window Proofreading.'" *Writing Lab Newsletter* 9, no. 9 (1985): 8–9.

Williams, Joseph M. "The Phenomenology of Error." *College Composition and Communication* 28 (1981): 152–68.

Witte, S. P., T. Miller, and L. Faigley. *A National Survey of College and University Program Directors.* Writing Assessment Project Technical Report no. 2. Austin: Univ. of Texas, 1982.

Wolfson, Nessa. "Compliments in Cross-Cultural Perspective." *TESOL Quarterly* 15 (1981): 117–24.

Writing Center Journal. Ed. Jeanette Harris and Joyce Kinkead. Logan, Utah: Utah State Univ.

Writing Lab Newsletter. Ed. Muriel Harris. West Lafayette, Ind.: Dept. of English, Purdue Univ.

Appendix A
Conference Excerpts

Excerpts 1 and 2 are reprinted from handouts distributed by Donald A. McAndrew and Thomas J. Reigstad at their Conference on College Composition and Communication postconvention workshop, "Training Tutors for Lab or Class" (March 31, 1984).

1. Roger Garrison conference, 11 April 1979

In the following conference, Roger Garrison is working with a student named Andrea, who is writing a news story about a jogging event to be held on her campus. As you read through the dialogue, consider the following:

1. What suggestions and recommendations does Garrison offer the writer?
2. What positive comments does Garrison offer?
3. What concerns does this student mention? Are her concerns considered by the instructor?
4. Compare this conference excerpt with excerpt 2, between Donald Murray and a student. How do Garrison and Murray differ in controlling the direction of the conference? Can you find comments by Garrison and Murray which illustrate the differences and similarities you notice?

Andrea: You said do something on public relations.

Garrison: Oh, yes.

Andrea: And I wrote it kind of like a newspaper. Is that, I didn't know if that's what you wanted or not.

Garrison: That's fine. Well, I think I suggested that to you.

Andrea: Yeah, you said something about a newspaper, but I didn't know if that's . . .

Garrison: Well, let's see how you've done this. [reads silently] Ah, this is for runners and joggers, isn't it?

Andrea: Um-hmm.

143

Garrison: Okay, I think I'd put that in the lead sentence if I were you. Because the title of the event is not entirely clear to the reader who knows nothing about the background of what you say, so when you say . . . "for runners and joggers," you're adding this information that the reader needs.

Andrea: Um-hmm.

Garrison: Now, here, take these two sentences and show me how you can save a couple of words here.

Andrea: "The race will . . ."

Garrison: Ah, the sentences themselves are perfectly all right. But I want you to see where you can save a couple of words.

Andrea: Okay, "After that later it will begin?"

Garrison: No. You can save two. See? [adds "-ing" to paper] "Beginning at."

Andrea: Okay.

Garrison: You make one sentence out of it instead of two. Okay?

Andrea: Okay. Um-hmm. I don't know if this should be, is that what they would call them, "entries"? The people, I couldn't think of . . .

Garrison: Yes. Actually, what I would do is, the entry blank, or something, has to be filled in?

Andrea: Yes.

Garrison: Well, then I would say, "entry *blanks.*" Okay?

Andrea: Well, this is the people who are already entered.

Garrison: Oh. Oh, no wonder you had a question about that! [laughter] No, then I would try something like this, "Those entered in the race should be . . ." Now where is, here, remember you're a reader here at the college, "each division—" what are the divisions? You're not sure?

Andrea: There's different ones, there's different age . . .

Garrison: Age groups?

Andrea: Yeah.

Garrison: Well, I think you can solve that either by first finding out what the divisions are . . .

Andrea: They are just different age groups. Would I have to mention age group divisions?

Garrison: Oh, all right. Then, I would help the reader . . . "age group divisions," fine. See because then that adjective qualifies that enough for a reader who doesn't know anything about it. To know this group by ages instead of whether you've got one-legged races, two-legged . . . [laughter]

Andrea: Okay.

Garrison: [pointing at closing phrase which reads "See you there!"] You never put that kind of thing in a piece like this. Okay?

Andrea: Yeah. I wasn't sure if I should or not.

Garrison: Now I want you to take it back and to tighten it up just a little bit more. If you can get any more significant information, particularly toward the beginning. For instance, the building at which they're going to meet would be useful. What building? And, or where on the campus? Are they going to meet in the cemetery where they're going to run, or what? I'm serious. The purpose of a news piece like this is to transmit information in the most economical fashion that you can. So you compress as much as you can into a short piece for newspaper use. Okay? In a newspaper, this would be about two inches long.

Andrea: Um-hmm.

Garrison: And don't recopy it. I want to see what you're doing in between the lines.

Andrea: All right.

Garrison: Okay?

2. Donald Murray conference, 17 April 1979

In this excerpt Donald Murray is working with a student who is writing an article he plans to submit to a national magazine. The excerpt included here is only the first part of the conference. As you read through the dialogue, consider the following:

1. In the conference the student clearly takes the initiative in the conversation. What concerns does he mention?

2. What methods does Murray use to respond to his concerns?

3. How would you describe the questions Murray asks the student to consider?

4. How would you feel if you were the student in this tutorial?

Murray: So, you said you were mad at me all weekend?

Mark: No, actually that was kind of an overstatement, just to dramatize the way I was feeling (laughter) when I came into school. I didn't give you much thought this weekend as far as doing the paper, but I, there was a few times when I said "What am I doing this for?" because I didn't like what was happening. I felt like you sent me 15 pages, which was—wow—it was over half the paper—just wiping it out.

Murray: Yeah. I wanted about 20 pages out. I said, out of 34, 35, I think.

Mark: Right, precisely. It was 35 plus a paragraph.

Murray: Yeah.

Mark: So when I, you know, got home and was just wiping out these sections and I found some that, yeah, when I trimmed them out, hey, you know, that really didn't . . . all it did was clutter it up.

Murray: Right.

Mark: But then there were other sections that, you know, if I wiped out even a little bit of it, I had to wipe out a whole section.

Murray: Right, right.

Mark: And that section was I thought, well, I won't say crucial because I don't know what is crucial and what isn't . . .

Murray: Yeah, yeah.

Mark: It was a very integral part of what I was trying to do in the paper. And I felt like a lot of that was kind of lost by just pasting things together.

Murray: So, you didn't do it?

Mark: Oh, I did it.

Murray: You did it?

Mark: Yeah. You told me to cut it down as much as I could—

Murray: —yeah, as much as you could, but you cut it down to 23 pages—

Mark: —to 23 pages.

Murray: Ten pages, eleven pages?

Mark: Ah, yeah, something like that.

Murray: Yeah. All right.

Mark: And I was crying at that. (laughter) As for when I started getting angry at you was when I was typing up this paper, which I typed up three times, three times before, and I had all these sheets of paper that were almost identical except that they were offset because I cut up before and I had to type these things all over again and I was doing a terrible job typing that day, and I broke a pencil against the wall, and left two dents in the wall where I had beaten my pencil (laughter), and that's when I was getting frustrated.

Murray: When you were retyping it like that, did you find any changes in voice or anything happening in your writing? Did any of your writing change when you typed it? Or, are you able to isolate yourself?

Mark: Phew! Boy, that's not the time to ask me on that one.

Murray: Yeah.

Mark: Because I was just not into it.

Murray: Yeah. What do you think of the piece now?

Mark: As it is now? I wasn't happy with it.

Murray: Yeah.

Mark: It seemed to be too . . . It didn't seem to be as continuous and as complete as the other one.

Murray: Yeah.

Mark: I feel like if I'm going to cut it down to 15 pages, I'm going to have to throw out the whole paper, and restructure and retype it.

Murray: Yeah.

Mark: And not try to say the same thing that I'm trying to say.

Murray: This merely was, as I said, arbitrary and it was also tentative, as you mentioned it was an experiment—

Mark: —which is why I might not even continue it.

Murray: —and you, you know, compromised halfway between, you're right in suggesting which way you were going to go. I think the piece is improved a lot. I really do.

Mark: (laughter) Okay. That's what I got to figure out with you, because I don't know exactly why you think it's improved. Or what you're saying—

Murray: —because it's a tighter, I've been pushing you to be freer
and let your voice come stronger, but I think it did run on
a bit. And I wanted it to. But I think that this tightens it
up and makes it a much better piece. I think it's a much
more focused, stronger piece. I have a couple of small
things in the beginning here, a couple of uses of language, then I saw practically just—well, see if I can find
them. I didn't want to mark this up because it's so beauti-
fully typed. A couple of words that I might . . . see where
they are. I think this is, you've given it much more focus,
and I really feel that the experience is more compressed. I
mean, you've got to decide that ultimately, and it's hard
for you to decide and it's hard for me to decide. Both of us
are bad readers in the sense we've read it several times—

Mark: —been reading it all along, um-hum.

Murray: —but it read much more of a whole, than the time before.
I did think it did run on too much, and I wanted you to
go on and on and on, you know, I talked to you at the
beginning about fifty or seventy-five pages, you turned
green at certain stages.

Mark: Yeah.

Murray: But I think that I really like it. But I think in the writing
there's just something that disappeared. Let me see if I
can find this, having brought that up, find out one or two
words.

Mark: I wanted to look over that introduction a bit. Because the
sentence structure seemed to be repetitive.

Murray: Yeah.

3. René's conference, 15 April 1985

In the excerpt included here, René, a peer tutor, and a student in the
writing lab where René works are meeting to talk about an assignment for his composition course. The student has brought along a list
of topics that the teacher has given the class. Initially, the student has
chosen the topic of learning from a mistake. He has brought to the
tutorial a draft of a paper which discusses several mistakes he has
made. The excerpt of the tutorial included here represents the first
quarter of the whole session. In a section not included here, about
halfway through the tutorial, the student decides to switch to a different topic from the list distributed by the teacher.

As you read through the excerpt, consider the following questions:

1. What is René trying to accomplish with this student?
2. How well does she succeed in achieving her goal(s)? What does she do or say that contributes to this?
3. To what degree does René control the direction of this tutorial? What evidence is there that the student voices his concerns?
4. What problems do you think the student is having with this paper? To what extent does he understand René's questions?
5. What goals would you set for this tutorial, and how would you achieve them?

René: Well, what kind did you pick? As in description, as in definition?

Student: It's like . . .

René: OK, first off, I really think you should limit your paper to one of these because it says your topic is learning from one mistake or from *a* mistake. One mistake, not learning from mistakes, OK? So, I think you should pick the one you can write the most about first of all, and then we can come up with some ideas for it, OK? Umm, I want to know how you broke your car. What were you doing? What do you mean by broke your car? I don't know how a person can break a car, OK? Pretend like I am from another planet and I know nothing about cars, so you have to tell me this. And it could be a very good descriptive paper about how you broke your car . . . because that's learning from a mistake, right?

Student: Yeah, but I mean like . . .

René: OK, tell me about what you did. Start from the beginning. You bought your new Chevette, right? That's what you say here. "I bought a brand new Chevette when I got my license." So you were sixteen, right?

Student: Yeah.

René: OK, so what did you do?

Student: I don't know, just . . .

René: Well, did you wreck it? Did you . . .

Student: No, but I just . . . give me a second . . .

René: What?

Student: Let me think.

René: OK, tell me like you're telling me a story. This is your Happy Hour or Story Hour, OK?

Student: I just like, like just drove it hard. I drove it real fast, you know, and I just . . .

René: Well, just give me a "for example."

Student: If I was at a stoplight, I had to beat the guy to the next stoplight. That's how I drove it hard.

René: Oh, so you're the rabbit instead of the turtle.

Student: Yeah.

René: OK . . .

Student: So, you know, I was pretty hard on it.

René: On your car. So wait, what eventually happened to the car though? I don't understand.

Student: OK, the clutch, I mean, I broke that.

René: You broke the clutch?

Student: Yeah. The reason I wouldn't tell you about, I mean . . .

René: You can tell me. What? What's so funny?

Student: How can I explain this here? Just a second. All right.

René: I want several instances, I mean, examples . . .

Student: No, no, just the clutch, man. I just broke that so . . . that's how it sort of happened.

René: See, OK, what I want you to do with this paper is I want you to give me the background of how . . . Well, do you want to work with that one or would you prefer to work with whatever this one is? Or you can work with the accident or the ticket. But I want you to concentrate on one of them and give me a lot of description and background of it. Exactly what happened. I want that kind of stuff. So you can use lots of adjectives, you know?

Student: Uh huh. Well, like, this stuff is just made up.

René: Oh, was it? OK.

Student: Well, I mean that guy, you know, you just make stories more interesting to everyone, you know. But this stuff really happened.

René: These last two were actually . . .

Student: Where I started talking about these two things.

René: OK. Well, which one do you think you can develop more fully? Which one do you think you can write more about? Because you've got to focus your paper on one of these because it's too broad right now, and it's not . . . I don't see you tying anything together. It's like here's one story, here's another story, and here's another story. And now you should bring it all into focus. Even if you want to work with this one you made up, if you can describe it and work on it . . .

Student: You mean, like, what do I describe about it?

René: Well, how to . . . I mean, you have to keep remembering this is about learning from a mistake. So you always have to go back to that no matter what story you develop in your paper. You always have to go "How did you learn from this mistake?" You have to tell me what the mistake was, the circumstances surrounding it, and how you learned from it.

Student: OK, this story that I made up, you know? Well, I intended . . . That kid, you know, is driving real reckless and everything, you know. Well, this older man is driving real careful. Then, down here where it says the old man . . .

René: . . . used to drive that way . . .

Student: Yeah. So he has already learned from his mistake.

René: He's learned, but the kid hasn't.

Student: Yeah, but he just now has.

René: You've got an interesting idea if you can develop it. If you want to work with that one, we can work with that one. But you've got to come up with . . . You have to have the focus of your paper, and then you have to have all the supports, and how you learned from the mistake. Because you have to remember that that's what the paper is all about. So, which one do you want to work with? Which one do you think you can be the most creative and tell me every single detail?

Student: What if we made this . . .

René: I don't know if you want . . . But, well, you can base factual material . . . You can give me lots of, uh, material. Well, I would think you could, for how you drove your car to break.

Student: I guess you had to be there.

René: I still don't know how you can break a car, but that's OK. Which one do you want to do? We have to sit down and develop, I mean really think about these things, and develop some . . .

Student: Hmmmm . . .

4. Tim's tutorial

The conference included here, from Joyce Kinkead's "Tutors in the Writing Center," 6–8, is from a writing lab tutorial. As you read the excerpt, consider the following questions:

1. What is Tim trying to accomplish in this tutorial?
2. To what extent does the student learn how to become a self-sufficient writer? Does the student voice any problems or concerns about the paper?
3. What methods and approaches does Tim use to help the student?
4. If you were the student, how would you react to this tutorial? Do you consider Tim an effective tutor? Why?

Tim: What was the assignment?

Student: It's supposed to be a definition essay, English 101.

Tim: OK, and what was your word?

Student: He said you could define a word or explain something.

Tim: Do you have any kind of outline for this?

Student: Well, kind of. I drew one.

Tim: OK, I'd like to see something more in the form of— something where you've got an intro and come to a conclusion.

Student: OK.

Tim: And then what you need is a theme, and that theme can be anything.

Student: Like the title I put? Modern Music is Not Noise.

Tim: I see. I could have sworn that said hot noise. All right then that will be your theme, modern music. Ah, I think that this is probably OK for that first paragraph. You might want to give their definition and then yours.

Student: So give . . .

Tim: So b and then a. Depending on how it works best for you. But then down here in your conclusion you're going to restate.

Student: What was said in the paper?

Tim: Yes, restate the theme and summarize. The trick in the conclusion is to not say the same things that you've already said but to go beyond that. So what we're going to do here is list reasons why modern music is not noise; not everyone likes the same thing; that's fine.

Student: Did I introduce the paper right?

Tim: I think so.

Student: See, he said introduce it and start off by giving examples, you know.

Tim: OK. This is where you're starting here, your second draft, right, and I'd say right down here is where you want— your last sentence of your intro should be a strong sentence, what you're going to talk about. This is a long intro, but I think that you're OK in that respect. OK, when you say courtesy, how would you say that relates?

Student: I think people should respect what other people like, I mean, not everyone is going to like the same thing.

Tim: I think maybe you need to—you've said people don't like the same things and I think courtesy is a part of that. Let's keep reading and see how it works. (reads)

Student: I missed a semicolon there and also a comma.

Tim: Well, or you could use the semicolon and get rid of the "also." That might sound better, just get rid of the "also." I think that maybe instead of courtesy you may have to defend your music.

Student: OK.

Tim: You know I see courtesy down here in your outline, but I don't really ever see it mentioned up here. I think it's just a question of structure; you need to get an outline you can live with.

Student: This is my outline, but he never stressed writing one.

Tim: As I say . . .

Student: I'm glad you're helping me with that, because I don't
            know how to use one.

Tim: Well, OK.

Student: And it's the end of the quarter.

Tim: Well, I think that this will work for you in terms of an
            intro and a conclusion, and what you've got to get here
            is a theme; it's got to be one theme, something you
            can support.

Student: That's true. I did that.

Tim: Yes, I think so. I think that these two turned out to be
            pretty close to the same thing. I think you'll want the
            "disagreeable sound" here and maybe you could even
            come up with—you're basing your whole paper really on
            this first paragraph, and I think you're going to have to
            try to defend your music a little more, rather than just
            your right to listen to what you want. You're saying that
            modern music is not noise. I would say think in terms of
            defending your music more.

Student: All right.

Tim: OK?

Student: Thank you.

Tim: Uh huh.

5. Kathy's conference, April, 1985

The excerpt included here is from a writing lab conference between
Kathy, a peer tutor, and a student with whom she has been working
for many weeks. In the excerpt included here, Kathy and the student
have been working for a while with an exercise on active verbs and are
now moving on to another exercise sheet on linking verbs.

As you read the excerpt, consider the following questions:

1. What is Kathy's purpose in asking the student if memorizing is
   easy for him? Why does she then tell him about her brother
   and sister?

2. To help the student remember linking verbs, Kathy uses several
   techniques. What are they?

3. Kathy has the student practice supplying different adjectives to
   complete the sentence "Apples are . . ." Why?

4. How well do you think Kathy has succeeded in accomplishing her goal of having this student learn to recognize linking verbs?

Kathy: OK, so that's fine. Now you really understand action verbs. We'll say, "OK, that's one thing we've really got down." OK?

Student: OK.

Kathy: Now at any time if I feel you're missing them. If you're not clear, we'll go back.

Student: Right.

Kathy: So, I think OK with action verbs. I'm pleased. You should be pleased with yourself, really. Good job. Verbs that show existence—another term is linking verbs, OK? You stop me when you want to ask questions or discuss it. (Reads from the exercise sheet.) "Not all verbs show action. Some verbs show that something exists or is related to something else. These verbs are called linking verbs. One group of these verbs consists of words like 'is.' These verbs are called verbs of being." Verbs of being . . . I want to make sure you know what it is.

Student: State of being.

Kathy: State of being. OK. Your cousin is in the room. Try to find, if there's a verb, try to find one for me. Where is it?

Student: Ahhh . . .

Kathy: OK, cousin . . . what?

Student: Umm, if it's not "is," it would be "in."

Kathy: OK, I'm saying this is the verb, and there isn't another one. So we're going to have to be able to recognize this. That's what I was trying to say. The cousin . . . doesn't say that he walked, doesn't say that he sat . . . He is in the room. I am here. That tells you something about me and what, you know, . . . that's what I am . . . I am here. The verb "is" tells us that the cousin exists. Doesn't tell us what he's doing in his existence. But we know that he is. Other verbs of this group include "am," "are," "was," and "were." Give me a two-word sentence with this.

Student: I am.

Kathy: I am.

Student: They are.

Kathy: They are.

Student: I was.

Kathy: I was, yeah.

Student: They were.

Kathy: They were. OK. Sometimes verbs like "is" connect or link two words or ideas. Let's not work on that yet. Let's work on this. Let's make sure we got this, OK? In terms of being . . . write down these verbs for me, would you? "Is," "am," "are," "was," and "were." How are you at memorizing things? Does memory work come easy for you? Or is it hard for you?

Student: It's hard.

Kathy: Hard, OK. My brother, David, he's fourteen. He's a freshman in high school, and he can memorize like that. It's, you know, easy for him. Kelly, who is ten . . . it's the hardest thing in the world for her. I'm sorta like her. So it, you know, doesn't . . . it just tells me something about them. It doesn't qualify them one way or the other . . . good, bad, better than, you know, anything like that. I wondered because, you know, one way we could approach things is to try to memorize them. So if that's not an easy tool for you, then we'll find something else.

Student: My chemistry. It's the same. I have lots to know, to memorize. My roommate, he makes lists to memorize, but that doesn't help me.

Kathy: Hmm . . . chemistry . . . So how do you study . . . to remember all that stuff?

Student: I write it down, sort of notes like, over . . . I write notes after lecture and from the book.

Kathy: Well, OK, so we can do the same thing here. I want you to be able to recognize them though. So, write them . . . good, that's fine . . . All right . . . And what else do you call them? Linking verbs and states of being. OK, I just want to go over this one more time. Tell me about the state of being.

Student: Shows its existence.

Kathy: Think of it. You've got a right to exist . . . you've got a right to be in that chair. You are. So let's go on here with the sheet. "Connect or link two words or ideas in a relationship." In other words, we're going to start over here with a person. We're going to have this linking verb in the middle, and then we're going to relate this person to the rest . . . this part of the sentence to the rest of this sentence. To the rest that's over here. It's gonna be like a balance. They may not be equal, but they're gonna be related. Apples are red. Now, apples don't equal red, but they're related. In that sentence, "are" connected them, linked them. It made some connection up here for me. Apples are yellow. I can relate those to each other.

Student: Apples are green.

Kathy: Apples are green. Apples are bitter. Come up with another.

Student: Apples are delicious.

Kathy: Apples are delicious. Apples are . . .

Student: Juicy.

Kathy: Juicy.

Student: Sweet.

Kathy: Apples are sweet. Apples are great . . . OK . . .

Student: Apples are amazing . . . (laughs)

Kathy: The amazing apple. (laughs)

Student: Well, you've got the incredible egg.

Kathy: Yeah. In each of those instances, this part was telling you about this part. They're related. There's a connection.

Student: And "are" was the connector.

6. Mickey's conference, April, 1985

The excerpt included here is from a writing lab tutorial between Mickey and a student whom she has met for the first time. In the portion of the transcript included here, they are working with the first paragraph of a paper the student has brought in . The paragraph they are discussing is as follows:

> Videos have unquestionably altered peoples relationship with music. At nightclubs across the country people dance to videos and after tiring with dancing, relax in the video lounges. Can people no longer listen to music on the radio when they watch and hear music on television? Stars such as Madonna and David Lee Roth have become successful largely on the strength of their videos. Because of the publics reaction to them videos have taken on a new importance in rock. Much controversy has arisen over whether this new development has hurt or helped rock music. Although evidence exists to support both sides, a careful review of the facts suggests that videos have not damaged rock music.

As you read the excerpt, consider the following questions:

1. What aspect of the paper does the writer want to work on? How do you know this?

2. What methods or approaches does Mickey use to help the student? What other techniques might have been used?

3. What changes is Mickey suggesting that the student make in the paragraph being considered? To what degree do you think the student understands how to take this paragraph home and rewrite it?

4. Would you characterize Mickey as an effective tutor? Why?

Mickey: I'm not quite sure I understand what you mean . . . that you're concerned that the paper doesn't follow like it should.

Student: Well, I'm not sure that the conclusions are right . . . that they follow correctly . . . whether it's balanced . . .

Mickey: Did your teacher make some comment about this?

Student: No, she said in my last paper I should watch especially to stay away from clichés. But this draft just doesn't go along smoothly. Maybe I'm having trouble with the topic.

Mickey: Would it help if we read this together? I could sort of tell you as we go what I'm getting from the paper as a reader . . . if I'm having trouble picking up your meaning. Maybe those are the spots that aren't smooth. OK?

Student: Sure, go on.

Mickey: Why don't you read the first few sentences out loud, and then we'll see where we are.

Student: "Videos have unquestionably altered peoples relationship with music." Ummm . . . I forgot the apostrophe. Hate them. It goes here, right. "Videos have unquestionably altered people's relationship with music. At nightclubs across the country people dance to videos and after tiring with dancing, relax in the video lounges. Can people no longer listen to music on the radio when they watch and hear music on television? Stars such as Madonna and David Lee Roth have become successful largely on the strength of their videos."

Mickey: Umm, I'm not quite sure here . . . let's see . . . You're talking about people watching and listening to videos.

Then, you go on to how people become successful. Is there a reason why there's a switch here? I'm not sure why or how I got here, about Madonna and David Lee Roth becoming successful.

Student: Because of the public's relation to them. Videos have taken on a new importance in rock. I want to show three different examples of how . . . of how videos are changing rock music.

Mickey: Three examples of how videos are changing rock music?

Student: Well, like altering people's relationship with it.

Mickey: Let me see if I see what you're saying. They alter people's relationship . . . because . . . people go to these video lounges.

Student: They don't dance to records anymore. They dance to like you know, these video screens and you no longer go into a quiet room, you go to a . . . you still watch music.

Mickey: Oh, I see! OK, the examples. I didn't quite understand. I see what you're saying now. They alter people's relationship with music. OK, the altering went from one thing to another.

Student: Right.

Mickey: So, now they're dancing to videos, but I don't know what it's changed from.

Student: Just records, you know.

Mickey: It would really help me as a reader if you showed me what it changed from—to. You've given the "to" side pretty clearly. Here's what it changed to, but I didn't see that this was an example of change. Let me give you an example. At nightclubs across the country, people no longer dance to records, they dance to videos. Then, I'd know the old, and I'd see the change to, the altering that you mention in the first sentence.

Student: OK, OK. I guess . . .

Mickey: See, I missed your point because I couldn't go from the "altering" in the first sentence to anything like that in the second sentence. And you wanted me to see this as an example.

Student: Right, right . . . I get your meaning.

Mickey: So, they used to dance to records, and now they dance to videos. So that's one thing . . . Now, here you want to add on another example, right?

Student: Sure.

Mickey: Have you talked about using transition words in class?

Student: Yeah.

Mickey: OK, so how if you're adding one thing to another, how do you signal to the reader?

Student: I don't really know.

Mickey: Sure you do. If you told me your room is painted white, and you also wanted to tell me it has three windows, what words would you use to show the connection?

Student: "And?"

Mickey: Sure, there are a lot of connectors like "and." What other words mean "and"?

Student: . . . You mean like "also"?

Mickey: Great. OK, so with that kind of clue, I would see that you're making a list here of examples. Now I know that one thing is they used to dance to records and now dance to videos. What else? What's next on your list of examples?

Student: Well, in addition, young people no longer listen to music on the radio, but they can watch and hear music on TV.

Mickey: Now we're rolling. Let's go on to this sentence. I don't know if it's going to explain that one some more, or if it's going to be a new thing on your list.

Student: It's like people now don't become good just because of their quality, but more on the quality of their videos rather than the quality of their sound.

Mickey: Yeah, I missed that point. See, you just did a lot of good explaining, but it's not there on the page. You're saying that they become successful on the strength of their videos. I was reading along and not really following what you were saying. So, now, those are three things. Because of the public's reaction to them, videos have taken on a new importance in rock.

Student: I thought that would sum up these. Like people react, you know, like people are having new reactions to videos.

Mickey: Then what about a summing-up word to show me that that's what you're doing.

Student: Could I say "to sum up"? I suppose since it's a conclusion, I could do something like "therefore," but that's kind of too formal. Maybe I could just explain that as a result . . .

Mickey: Hey, that's great. Now you're really meshing ideas and sentences together for me.

Appendix B
Practice Activities

I. Appropriate and Inappropriate Comments

A. Would an effective tutor make these comments to a student? Why?

1. You've got a comma splice in that sentence. The reason is that you've got two independent clauses separated by a comma. You can either add the word "but" here or separate the clauses into two sentences. I think it would be best to leave it as one sentence with that coordinating conjunction.

2. OK. So what you've got so far is a mess. Here's how you need to fix it up . . .

3. You say this is a revised version of your paper? Let's start by looking at what you've got. Let's read it through together.

4. This is an excellent paragraph! All it needs are a few more details. Put something more after that sentence there about how the locker room smells, something perhaps about the smell of sweat in the air and damp sneakers. And maybe the smell of Bactine and bandages. That will definitely improve it.

5. If I understand what you're saying, you think that the paper doesn't flow smoothly enough but that you don't know what to do about fixing it. Is that what you think is the weakest part of the paper?

6. So this is your first draft? OK. One thing that I can see that needs fixing up is the spelling. Let's start by looking for misspelled words.

7. You say that flying in a glider is a special kind of feeling. That's interesting. I've heard that gliding is a magnificent sport, but I don't know much about it. Could you tell me more about this feeling? What's it like?

8. This draft is quite good. The point you wanted to make here was that gun control is an infringement of people's rights. What you need to do to make that sentence clearer is to tell the reader

more overtly, something like "Making laws about owning guns infringes on people's rights" and then go ahead and explain why.

9. As I listened to you reading your paper, I could hear how much you really like surfing, but I'm not sure why you're writing this paper. Is it to convince people who've never surfed to try it? Or, perhaps, are you mainly interested in telling us why you like surfing?

10. I'm glad we have this chance to talk because I'll need to explain a lot of things before you write your next draft. You've got a bunch of comma errors, there's some verb tense switching, your thesis statement needs to be narrowed, and we better rework this third paragraph. It's pretty short. Oh yes, I saw some spelling errors, and I bet your teacher wanted more descriptive details if this is a narrative. Yeah. I think it's a narrative. Am I right? What was the assignment? So, let's see, first you need to know the difference between "their" and "there" . . .

11. It says here on the referral sheet that your teacher wants you to work on using articles. Articles are the words "the," "a," and "an" that go in front of nouns. Do you have markers like these in your native language?

12. I'm having trouble understanding why this third sentence in that paragraph comes after the second one. Could you help me see the connection by telling me what you wanted to write here?

13. So, we're going to do some work on commas now. There are a couple of ways we could start, depending on how you think you'd learn best. Do you like to work with formulas? We could work out some formulas. Or should we start by looking at the sentences in your paper? I could give you the rule, and you could try applying it to your sentences.

14. *Tutor:* So you think you want to write about why vacations at the beach are boring. Why *is* this kind of vacation so boring? Have you been to the beach lately? . . . *Student:* Yeah, we went there for a week last summer. There was no place to hang around in the evenings . . . *Tutor:* Really? Well, that's a good point to make for your paper. Nothing to do when it rains. Let me just write that down here . . . What else bugs you about being at the beach for a few weeks?

15. Is this your best effort? If I were you, I'd start a littler earlier next time. Waiting until the night before it's due is just a mistake. You can't get a paper done that fast. No way. What are we supposed to do now if you have to hand it in this afternoon? Correcting the grammar isn't really going to help much. Sorry.

16. I can see that you have a very full outline, but maybe it might be best for you not to start with outlines if you feel so weighed down by them. Have you tried free-writing as a way to start? Here, let me show you how to use this as a way to get your ideas flowing. Give me a topic, something you've had in class lately, and I'll try to do some free-writing and see how it goes.

17. Look at this sentence here. Do you see anything wrong? Try reading it out loud and sort of listen to yourself as you read. Does it sound OK?

18. Yeah, I sympathize. I've had that problem too, especially when all my material is on a bunch of notecards scattered all over my desk. Have you ever tried just sorting them into piles and trying to make an outline from the categories you set up for your piles? Sometimes that works for me.

B. *What would an effective tutor say to a student who made these comments?*

1. Could you show me what's wrong here? I know this paper isn't very good, but I don't know what to do to improve it.

2. My teacher told me to come in and get some help, so I'm here. Personally, I don't like writing. I just want to get through this course, and then I'm done with English. I'm an ag major, and we don't have to do any writing.

3. Well, I don't know. Should I put in that part about my mother going back to school? Maybe it's better without that? Or should I explain why she lost her job? Will that help? I wanted to add some biographical stuff about her, but I couldn't decide if it belongs here.

4. OK, so you said that the introduction should explain my purpose. And you said to leave this sentence out. OK. You want a transition here too. Right?

5. Everything I write, he hates. Man, if I handed in the Declaration of Independence, he'd find something wrong with it. Maybe I should just try to switch into someone else's class. He'll never give me anything higher than a *C* no matter how much I improve.

II. Sample Student Sentences

What problems are evident in the following examples from student writing? What diagnostic questions would help to determine the instruction to be offered? What topics of instruction might be offered, and what strategies might be used?

1. My favorite music is really the absolute best you can listen to because I think that it puts you in your own world when you listen to it.

2. We went swimming in a lake and I stepped on an earring and I started to cry so I had to go to the doctor to get it pulled out.

3. Their are 3 people I admire the most Kathleen, Midge, and Heather. They are always fun to be with and to talk to which is a favorite activity of ours. We get along perfectly and we never fight. But what I like and in my own personal opinion I think are group is the best.

4. Many people feel that death is unspeakable, a horrible thing that is not to be discussed. Something to be fought.

5. The first flaw I see in the essay on Agression and Violence is confussing information. The essay is confussing in 2 different ways. The ways it is confussing are the talk about homo sapiens and Choukoutien man. What was so confussing was I never knew man was first a homo sapien. I thought man started out liking women. And later began to turn to men. It is very confussing to imagine man as being gay before civilization came along. How could the world be populated if men were homo sapiens first. This concept is very strange and foriegn to me.

6. Then I play video games and play Space Invaders and Mrs. Packman then I play Cinipeed then I shut it off and play with our computer.

7. Working out and buying new running clothes and neat looking shoes is not going to make you fast, only hard work and preperation will do it, there are no short cuts. . . . Eat right is very important when running and exercise is involved.

8. Research shows that wife beaters come in every size, income status, and color. After investigating many reports they show that persons taking part in such conflicts are of all ages.

9. My brothers have clashing identities. First, Pat is the kind of brother you see on television. The kind of brother that would help you on your homework or maybe the brother that has the a good looking girlfriend, which Pat has all these qualities. Randy, on the other hand, isn't the smartest brother in the world but, he's been around and knows a lot. The best summery of Randy is that he's the Mr. Hyde of Pat. As for advice Randy convinced me to go to college.

10. A room can show a person's likes or dislikes. I really hate the process of cleaning. But the after result of organization is worth it. When friends come over, it is an occasion that the room gets cleaned.

11. On my first appearance at campus I noticed the poor quality of living quarters occupied by students. This made up part of my decision on why I hate dorms and housing units.

12. My hometown lacks many parks and recreation centers and because of this it makes it a bad place to rise children. Without having any parks there is no real safe place for kids to play. Having no parks or any type of center where kids can play games or swim, leaves the kids bored and angry. The kids could find trouble playing in the streets and they might even get into vandalism.

13. I use to smoke cigarrettes alot, and an occasional cigar as well, but after they started putting the warning from the Surgeon general on all the packs I decided to stop. Missing it's great flavor, tobacco chewing was the natural replacement for smoking for me. Now I still recieve all the pleasure of tobacco without the risk of recieving cancer to.

14. I started to have English in elementary school. English taught in the six years of elementary was swallowed. There was not emphasis in writing composition. In high school English had became one of the important subjects in class. Composition is given twice a week. Due to number of students in class, the teacher was not able to concentrate on every students. Some of the students had better English standard that the ones who were not good were quite difficult to catch up during lessons.

15. The irony is that Jonathan Swift fail to embarrass the imagine of the Irishmen but make up for it by shaming the imagine of the Irishwomen. . . . It is the respondible of the parents or parent to take care of their children.

III. Sample Student Papers

On the following pages are samples of student writing. As you read through these papers, you can either use the paragraph of comments and questions about that paper to guide you in thinking about a conference with that student, or you can ask yourself the following general set of questions.

What are the strengths and weaknesses of the paper?

What questions would you ask the student at the beginning of the tutorial?

What predictions would you make about the answers you'd get to the questions you've just formulated?

Keeping in mind the fact that you don't have any input from the writer and can only work from your predictions, make a tentative list of your goals for the first conference with this student.

What strategies might you use to accomplish those goals?

What would you say and do at the beginning of the tutorial?

If you can, work with another tutor willing to role-play the writer of this paper and conduct a mock tutorial.

1. Jack's paper

As you read this paper, it's likely that what you'll notice first are all the grammatical errors. However, Jack's paper is not yet ready for work on editing skills because it needs revising that will make the focus or main point clearer. In the present draft the opening and closing sentences state that Jack is writing about what he gains from walking, though the middle portion of the paragraph describes what he sees while walking. What strategies might you use to help Jack unify his paper? What strengths do you note in the paper that you might comment on? When it's time to begin work on grammar and mechanics, what are the major areas Jack needs to work on?

Jack

The activity that I find myself doing to relax & unwind is a slow walk. I usually perform this action when I am upset, either at myself or someone I am acquainted with. I sometimes walk for a couple of hours, just thinking about my problems, and alot of the time I do find myself having a pretty good conversation with myself. When I'm walking I notice alot of things about people. I see flowers, trees and a lot of other natural sights. Such as the wildlife. I think my biggest focusing point when I'm walking and thinking is the sky. It is so beautiful no matter what state it is in. On a bright sunny day it is a fascinating light blue, but on a windy, stormy day it is a very fluffy, gray, low hanging bunch of pillows. As I walk I feel the wind zip through me, the rough pavement beneath my feet, and the unraveled strings in my pockets. I hear an occasional sigh from deep within myself as my voice echoes off the seasoned air and reflects my verbal thoughts back to me. My sense of smell is usually focused on the clean freshness of the country air, but it is tampered with sometimes by the sweet smell of a patch of wild flowers. My walks really make me understand myself and most of the time I feel relaxed upon returning home again.

2. Eric's paper

When Eric appears with this paper, he seems very pleased with his effort and with the results. What comments might you make initially to him? After reading Eric's paper, you note that it needs to be revised so that his arguments are more clearly stated and supported in each paragraph. Since the organization and development of the ideas in this paper are weak, how would you help Eric improve the paper? What are some of the strengths of the paper that you'd comment on?

Science or Humanity

Animals are killed for many different reasons. Some of the reasons animals are killed are for the sport, fun, and research. Often people hunt animals for the fur, meat, or just for the adventure. Research using drugs on animals is necessary for the advancement of human knowledge and life.

but the methods used are extremely
cruel. Without using animals for
experiments, either diseases would
go uncured or humans would have
to be used in experiments. Experiments
with radiation and cancer could
not be conducted if scientists did
not use animals. People would
protest if experiments were run
on human beings. If the same
number of humans were killed
as the number of rats and rabbits
that are killed there would not
be a housing and food shortage
on the earth. Cruelty to animals
in the name of science should
be prohibited.

Many animals are killed and
cut up in very cruel ways.
Often five hundred rabbits are
killed and the liver removed from
each rabbit, and the remaining
body parts are thrown away.
Then the experiments are run on
the livers. While a nearby
laboratory runs a behavior test
on six hundred rabbits. Then they
take the rabbits, and kill them
and remove only the lung from
the rabbit and throw the rest
of the rabbit away. The laboratory
assistants then do the experiments
on the lungs. The two laboratories
together kill one thousand one
hundred rabbits. When they could

have worked together and killed
only six hundred rabbits.

The methods used to kill
rats and rabbits that scientists
and laboratory workers are
inhumane and sometimes these methods
are very cruel. some laboratories
on certain days kill many
animals of the same type on
that day for example the
laboratory might have rabbit
day. One way to kill a rat
is to hold it by the tail and
the rat's head on ~~the~~ a nearby
table. Another way to kill
a rat is to hit the rat over
the head with a solid lead pipe.
The neat way to kill a rat
is to take a rat knock the
rat out and then use a
guillotine to cut the rat's head
off. The guillotine is mainly
used to obtain brain tissue. The
methods used in laboratories are
sometimes more cruel than they
should or have to be.

Many scientists kill an
animal and say it is just a
stupid animal with no feelings.
All animals have there own
way of life, however it might
be comared to the life ~~of~~ humans
go through. Without a doubt
people and scientists will
eventually realize all animals

that are killed or hurt are
living beings, that can think,
reason, and communicate in their
own way. The animals can also
feel the pain and agony that
scientists put them through all
in the name of science. All
animals must learn something
in there ~~life~~ life, no animal is
born knowing completely how
to live the animal life.

Millions of animals are put
through pain and agony each
year, all in the name of science.
Scientists should cut down on the
number of animals killed by
scientists today. If a scientist
removes one organ in one
laboratory and then sends the
body to another laboratory that
could use an organ not already
removed from the animals
body, this would eliminate the
need to kill so many animals.
At the same time scientists
should find ways that are not
as cruel as the methods used
now to kill animals. Scientists
should also find ways of lowering
the cost of preforming tests on
animals and parts of animals. If
the methods used to kill the animals
and the methods used do not change
then there will be many problems
scientists and laboratories will have
to face.

                    Eric

3. Fran's paper

As a reader, how do you react to Fran's descriptions? If you find the word choices and details vivid, what comments might you offer to Fran as positive feedback? Also, since Fran's paper has several possible topics, how would you help her see the problem? If you were also an avid Nordic skier, would you mention your interest to her? Why?

Fran

Exhaling a cloud of frosty smoke I push off to continue my nordic skiing. This demanding sport is of the same rigorous nature as swimming or running.

As I ski through the great stands of timber, sweat pours from my body traveling to the outer layer of clothing where it freezes in a frosted crust. My muscles pull and strain while I gasp for breath. On and on I go making loud sucking sounds when I pull in ice cold air to my lungs. A spray of tiny snowflakes hits my red and windburned face with enough velocity to cause a dull sting. Rhythmic movement makes my skis go clap - clap as they hit the snow.

As I support my upper body with my long blue poles, I scan the view from atop a relatively small mountain in the Rockies. The scene can not compare to the static and unsensual postcard scene. The light tint of blue in the crisp Colorado sky spues out a never ending supply of powder tht eventually covers this great range several feet deep. Mountains which seem to have sprouted everywhere seem only several city blocks distance are actually five to ten miles away. Dense pine forests covered with the precipitation are like thick hairs on a well developed beard.

Truly our ties with the natural and unspoiled are as deep rooted as the aspen in the ground. As man's exploits continue, his bonds become more and more weakened. Our fast paced society demands so much of us that we must return to the land and discover our essential elements.

4. Steve's paper

Steve has obviously worked hard on using specific detail here. Which of his details are especially effective? What comments might you make to Steve that would be both positive and helpful? Since the next-to-last sentence is not entirely clear to the reader, how could you help Steve to recognize the problem and to revise that sentence?

Who Am I?

I am the big burly line man on Frontier's football squad, holding out North White's biggest line men. I am the salty sweat rolling down my dirty face while tackling the running back and keeping him from scoring a touchdown. I am the blood from my hand after being cleated by the running back. I am the little boy inside of me crying with pain when the doctor stitches my hand up. I am the sore legs after running two laps around the track, then running 2 100's. I am the sand that gets in my shoes and socks. I am the basketball being bounced on the floor several times a game. I am the net on a basketball rim after every time someone swishes it, I turn in to a ring of fire. I'll be what I am for the rest of my life.

Steve

5. Janet's paper

What strengths do you notice in this paper? Since Janet's paper does have some problems with organization and with the major points that support her main point, one way to help her see this would be to offer her some sense of the disparity between what the reader expects to read next and what each paragraph actually discusses. What other strategies might help Janet revise this paper? If Janet appeared very unsure of her writing skills and kept asking questions such as "What do you want me to put here?" or "Is this sentence OK?" what would you say or do to help her?

Janet

More Punishment for Criminals

Criminals are people who break the laws and restrictions made by the government. If someone breaks the law, that person may or may not be punished. Criminals find out what their punishment will be in a court of law; therefore, laws are supposed to be carried out by the judge. Many criminals do not get enough punishment to stop them from committing crimes. For example, last year a high school student is caught with drugs on the school bus. This person is kicked out of school for the rest of the year, yet her parents did not punish her, she was not turned into the police. This person is still using drugs, and she is breaking the law. There should be more punishment for criminals in the United States.

Criminals are hurting thousands of victims every day. Criminals break into houses, rape people, and vandalize. There are many more crimes that hurt thousands of people, sometimes for life. Some victims of a crime cannot go on with their lives. If a woman has been raped, she has to live with that; also, she has to worry about it happening to other girls and women. If someone's house has been broken into, that family may not want to live in that house because of scary memories. If a house is burnt down, that family will never be the same. Joyous occurrances at that house, which is burned down, will not seem so joyous any more.

Too many criminals do not get punished severly enough to keep them hurting other people.

For example, if a young woman is raped, the police may find the man who raped the girl. After all the law suits and controversy, the judge may decide it is the man's first offense, so he will not get punished too severly. The results are, he has five months to a year in jail. This is not going to keep this man from doing the same thing to another girl or maybe the same girl when he gets out of jail. Rape is much worse than stealing, but sometimes the person who is caught stealing will get a more severe punishment.

Children's lives are influenced by television shows which show famous athletes or movie stars breaking the law. Young children see crime happening all over, on television, in their towns, just all around them. Children and teenagers see these athletes or movie stars breaking the law so they think it is all right for them to

do the same. For instance, a five to
seven year old may watch something like
"The A Team." The child will sit there
and watch all this violence. These shows
can affect the child as he grows, and he or
she may do something that could ruin that
child's whole life.

If new, stricter laws could be passed the
number of crimes should decrease. If new
laws are passed, criminals will get complete
punishment and hopefully learn that what
they are doing is wrong. If new laws are
not being passed, more victims will be
approached and endangered. Also, if laws
are not being passed, criminals will
continue crimes. Parents should set up an
organization to learn how to stop their
children from becoming a criminal. If
this organization could become a law, there
will be fewer criminals throughout the
world. Action has got to be taken to stop
criminals throughout the world.

6. Jon's paper

What positive comments might you make to Jon at the beginning of
the conference? Since his paper needs more specific details and examples, how might you help him see the problem and then generate
details to add to the paper? If Jon didn't seem too interested in
revising this draft, what might you say to help motivate him?

Jon

Car Model Building is a Very skillful Hobby

There are many skilled people out in
the world today. Unfortunately most of
these people apply there skills to hard

manual labor on the job; I have a way
for skilled people to apply themselves
while having fun. The fun I'm speaking
of is building model cars.

There are many reasons that make
building model cars a fun and rewarding
experience. This is a good hobby that many
people enjoy for relaxation or just to relieve
their boring moments of life. Either reason,
building models can give a person's mind
a chance to forget some major problems and
concentrate on something refreshing. Another reason to build models is for the good
feeling you receive from seeing a finished
project. It's very rewarding to see a solid
piece of proof on where a person's time was
consumed, and a good completed model car
can prove just where that time has gone.

So the next time you are at a store,
pick up a six-pack of your favorite
soda and a car model to build. Book right
home and while you are drinking your soda,
try and put a model together. It will
be a lot of fun.

7. Mary's paper

If Mary came to you for help with this paper but seemed unhappy
with what she had written so far, what questions or comments might
you start the conference conversation with? How could you help Mary
see that the first few paragraphs of this paper are not really relevant
and ought to be omitted? When Mary is ready to work on a final
polishing of her last draft, there will probably still be some grammatical problems to attend to. Using this draft as a guide, what does
Mary need help with?

Mary

Everybody hears it at some time in
their life. It is an old saying and it goes
something like this; you do not realize
how good you have ~~something~~ until you
do not have it anymore. This word, good,
can mean a number of things. It can mean
a feeling, a compliment or how well off
you are. When you leave home there are
a number of things you loose. You loose
the security of people taking care of you
and the familiar group that you always
hung around with. Besides from loosing
security, you leave the familiar surroundings
of home to move into a dorm room.

Boy, dorm life. I remember the dreams
that I had. The adventure of living on my
own. Well, almost on my own. I got the
roomate everyone warns you of. Actually, she
is not half as bad as they said she would
be. Besides getting a roomate, the university
makes it a point to tell you that group living
can add a significant dimension to your
total educational experience. Not only do it add
dimension to your educational experience.
Not only does it add dimension to your
education but the dorm is supposed to be
your home away from home. I tend to
wonder about this statement. Being
a new student away from home for more
than a week I tended to notice the things
I no longer have.

Being on your own is one trait you develop at college. There is no more of mom to pick up after me. To buy my shampoo or to wash my clothes. I get to make my own decisions and decide how active I am going to be. Making my own decisions is not always true. The dorms have rules that we must live with. Rules are great for the consideration of others but if we are adults then some of these rules need to be changed or slightly altered.

A rule that I have had a hard time adjusting to has been the rule of no warm blooded pets. According to the Board of Health rules, pets of these types are problems for sanitation. Alot of my friends and I find this funny. If they are sanitation problems than our houses and many others are breaking sanitation rules. I had always wondered why the university did not have at least one dorm pet owners. In my opinion, if pet owners could bring their pets, some of pressure of the day would be gone. It is proven that if you have something to worry you tend to forget or to put to ease the problem of the day. I also think that it would be easier to leave for college if the student did not leave their pet behind. That cute little, pudgy face surrounded by a ball of fur that would always come up to me and lay on my lap whether I wanted it to or not. So having at least one dorm for pet owners could make it home for them without being inconsiderate of others.

Another rule is that we are not allowed to have candles in our rooms. It is supposedly a fire hazard because of the open flame. People are allowed to smoke and this is just as bad of a fire hazard. People who smoke can drop their match, have their lighter blow up or even fall asleep smoking just as easily as someone knocking over a candle. I think that if other people smoke, even against the wishes of others, that we should be allowed to have candles. After all most of our houses have them.

Being at college can be a new experience and teach you how to be on your own but being in a dorm does not always feel like home. I think that if students are allowed to bring their pets and have the enjoyment of candles can make them feel a little more at home. After all the parents are paying for their best education and experience for their children and the child should be happy.

8. Heidi's paper

Heidi obviously likes cats and, as she immediately tells you, has a great deal more she'd like to add to this paper. However, the paper already strays from the assigned topic, why she likes cats. How would you help her develop a more unified paper?

Cats

I love cats. They can be so much fun to play with. With my cats I used to get a ball of string and send it rolling across the floor. Then my cat would go after it rolling and stumbling right along with it. I remember when she had kittens. They were so cute and furry. She took all the kittens, the <u>first</u> day, and put them under my bed. She would only let me pet them or hold them.

It is interesting how mother cats protect their young for about two weeks and then just ignore them. They care for them teaching them to care for themselves and maybe when their not ready to take care of themselves the mother leaves them.

There are many kinds of cats. I think the prettiest kind of cats are the tiger-striped ~~taby~~ cat. Most of them are very ~~play fu~~ playfull and well-behaved. With most people kittens are probably the most popular because they are friskier and funner to play with.

Cats are warm, furry, playful and prettiest They can be alot of fun

Heidi

9. Dan's paper

This is the third paper of Dan's that you've read, and once again, it is evident that he has worked hard to write an organized, well-developed paper. However, he wants to be an even better writer and wants to revise this draft, though, as he says, he doesn't quite know what's lacking. What positive comments might you offer him that would also be helpful to him? How would you get him to notice a few rough spots, such as the last sentence of the second paragraph, so that he can revise them?

Exercise The Mind

School time around the world is used for educating students to different subjects. Students in America generally are required to spend eight or nine hours a day in school during

weekdays. A student attends from six to nine different classes
a day. During school, there comes a need to remember knowledge
a student learns. A student needs to actually take home a part
of school in order to absorb the classwork. When homework is
given, some students complain, but their complaints are
unjustifiable. The value of homework should make it mandatory
in the Tippecanoe School Corporation(TSC).

Homework is a helpful way to study for a class. There is
not enough time in a school day for a student to learn everything
he should know, so homework gives a student that extra time to
learn. Doing homework helps students receive higher scores in
school. Therefore, it is relatively safe to say that going
over the work of the class gives a student a better knowledge
of it. Homework makes the student initiate research on his
own. Even when conferring with friends and reading books,
encyclopedias, and dictionaries, a student is making use of
inquiry. This may create a tendency for better reading skills,
which would benefit other classes in the respect of the practice
of reading it creates and an increased vocabulary.

Homework has the ability to teach a student independence
and individuality in school and life. Homework gives a student
the chance to express her own feelings or ideas on a subject
in written form. It develops in her a favorful character
toward achievement. It creates responsibility in the form
of wanting to achieve high grades. Homework forms a bond
between the student and teacher, and it also shows how well a
student grasps an idea. By the way a student answers a question,
her own distinct and personal views may be shown. Many times a
student who seems to do an ordinary job in some classes may

be found to be exceptional in classes that encourage new concepts or imagination. Homework gives a student the chance to be an individual.

The positive affect of homework creates an important impact on the future of a student's life. The loyalty, patience, and responsibility learned while doing homework are beneficial to ones life. Admirable work habits in school may carry over to how well a person works at his occupation. A student used to working hard and using all materials will generally use these skills at his job, as contrasted to a student who does not make use of all resources. The discipline which homework brings about stays with a person all of his life. Today's world is highly technological and fast changing. The habits derived from homework help a person keep step with the ever-changing world.

Action should be taken immediately if this county's students are to progress academically. If teachers are lax in their use of homework as a study guide in the class that they teach, not much will be gained from that class by the students. The main function of school is to teach students, and homework is an opportunity to have the affect of a teacher at home. The idea of classes alternating nights on which homework is assigned would appeal to most all students and teachers. Such suggestions should be made to the Tippecanoe School Corporation Superintendent. A proposal to work this homework alternation system in Indiana and the United States may be feasible. Other countries may follow the lead on public school policies.

10. *Traci's paper*

Traci was supposed to hand this in last week and tells you, by way of explanation, that she was sick for a few days and then had to make up some other work. She obviously doesn't have much time to work on revising this paper, but it lacks a clear focus or main point. How could you help her see the lack of unity? How could you also help to convince her that the paper is not yet done and needs more time and effort? Other problems that you notice are paragraphs which are inadequately developed. Would you mention that too? If so, how could you help her with that? Do you think Traci proofread this paper before giving it to you to read? How could you find out? How would you decide which of the many grammatical errors Traci should work on first?

An Expensive Good Time

As students pack their bags with suntan oil and swim-suits, some din't realize how expensive their spring break entertainment can be until they arrive back to school with an empty wallet.

In March college students fancy to turn to thoughts of Florida. At old-favorite resorts like Ft. Lauderdale. They seek warmth,companionship,and almost always ,beer.

Besides the amount of money it takes to get to a students favorite destination, which can range from $89   ' ,by car, or if a student would rather leave it to a party bus, it would cost approximately $179 ·   :. They advertise these as "The best prices" Many students,however, take the more convenient route, a few hours on a plane. This could range anywhere from $100 to $400 dollars depending on the class the student decides to take.

It's bad enough the price of getting to Florida but once the students hit the Florida line their mein concern is to hit the famous Lauderdale strip. This three mile strip is a minage of restaurants,bars and novalty stores. Students seem to be more attracted to the more famous bars, such as Penrods, patiently waiting in mile long lines not even concerned with the $10 dollar cover charge. The benefit of this cover charge includes a free t-shirt, a mug and all the food you can eat and

drink within and hours time. After waiting outside you are
faced with the massive humaities inside. Continuously waiting
in in all these different lines to receive your food or drink,
one never receives their full value of their money. If you
are a student who is lucky enough to make it to the bar , you
you must be waving a dollar before the bartender will even
consider filling up your mug.

No matter how much a student can drink they are still
faced with the empty stomach. To eat on the strip is another
added expense. The demand for food causes the little stands
along the strip to boost their prices during spring break.
Many students bring coolers of lunchmeat and snacks for the ride
down but once on the strip they have no choice but to pay the high
prices. A typical meal on the strip could range from $3.00
at a McDonalds to $20.00   ● at a decent restaurant.

Before students leave the sunny beaches of Lauderdale
theymust have some type of a remembrance such as a shirt,hat
or pin saying Ft. Lauderdale on it somewhere. The last couple
of days you can see students spending their last travelors check
or scrapping pockets for that last dollar. To buy a shirt or
sweatshirt can be one thing,but many students go overboard and
buy many useless things such as keychains and huggers. They
could spend as much as $20.00 ʌ in one souvenir shop.

Spring Break can be a great time but once they get back
to school, what do they have besides a Florida tan and a few
t-shirts.

Many students come back, look back at all the memories of
break and say to themselves, "Boy what an expensive good time."

11. Michael's paper

Having worked with Michael before, you know that he's a good writer
who writes easily. You also know that he's used to getting good
grades on his papers and doesn't want to revise his first drafts. What
comments might you make that would be helpful and would also let
him know that you too think this is a good paper? Also, since Michael
needs help with proofreading (which he doesn't do) and with that
long second paragraph, what strategies would you use to help him?

WHAT IS EXPECTED OF ME

All throughout my life, people have expected a lot out of me. Whether it be good grades, a clean room, or just being polite. But some of the things I have do are just plain STUPID!

For beginners, I get up every morning, at 6:00. Then I go and take a shower, which for is an accomplishment because I like to oversleep on occasion. But anyway, I always use a wash cloth to wash with. And at the end of every shower, it's always pretty wet, so I wring it out, and put it on the customary ledge, that the shower making company so nicely puts there for soap and various other things. Now I see nothing wrong with it, because every morning, right in the middle of my breakfast, my mother yells down the stairs saying, and I quote, "Get up here and hang up this washrag!" Now I'v not only got to hang up the washrag, but I've also got to clean up all of the milk that I spit out, when she scared me half to death! I clean up the milk and go upstairs. When I get there, all she is doing is standing there staring me right in the eye like Clint Eastwood would do right before he finished you off. After the stareing contest is over she utters, "Well are you gong to pick it up or am I going to have to get your father?!" Then comes the immortal debate, "Why?" "One!" "Mom!" "Two!" "All right...All right, but I don't see why I have to. After all it"s not hurting anyone." "It'll sour!" She says. Now there are three people in our household, not counting the dog, that use the shower. With this many people using the shower at different times of the day, hw can it sour!!! Every once in a while I pick it up and sniff it to see if it smells. It doesn't.

There is another thing that ranks right up there with the washcloth. It's having to go downstairs, into the kitchen, open the cabinet door, and take out the garbage,

right in the middle of my favorite T.V. show, "Mr. Wizard's
World." Now I don't know about you, but this also is one of
my most hated things. My mom will be downstairs sitting on
the couch, watching her favorite show, "Entertainment
Topnight." Out of nowhere, comes this horrible screem, "Get
down here and empty the garbage." Now I do admit that I am
supposed to empty the garbage when it gets full. But thats
no reason to make me go downstairs, go into the kitchen,
open the cabinet door, and take out the garbage, right in
the middle of my favorite T.V. show, "Mr. Wizards World."

     The third thing that really stirrs my Irish, is when
it's saturday morning, and I'm still in bed. My mother
comes upstairs, opens my door, and yells at me like a drill
seargent would on the first morning of basic training. The
reason she is yelling, is far beyond me, but she seeems to
know why she is. After she is done yelling, she leaves,
shuts the door, and I go back to sleep. I never even heard
a word she said. Then later she comes back upstairs and
wakes me up again. Then she makes me get up, go downstairs
and build a fire. She's been downstairs all morning now
watching T.V., and being lazy, so lazy she couldn't build a
fire! I just don't see why I should have to build the fire
when I'm just goig to back to bed afterwards.

     Like I said before, there are some things I don't mind
doing, but there are so9me things that really bother me a
lot. I see no reason for me to do these things, they're
just plain STUPID!

12. Kay's paper

Before Kay lets you read this paper, she tells you that it's awful
because she didn't know what to write and, besides, she says, she's a
terrible writer. How would you respond in a helpful manner to her
comments? After you read the paper, you see that it does need a lot of
work since many of the sentences do not support her main point.

What strategies would you use that would help Kay eliminate irrelevant sentences and that would help her see the need for more explanation in some of her other sentences? How would you do that in a manner that would also help Kay overcome her negative view of her writing skills?

Kay

Senior Composition Class

The purpose of English Composition is to help students enrich their writing skills. The students read several books throughout the year such as Brave New World. This book involves how our world might be in the future. The The student also learned about composition constituents, which later helped them write their research paper.

The research paper is the final paper which is due at the end of the semester. Mrs. Byland, the English Composition teacher required the students to have a seven to ten page typed research paper. Failure to turn in a research paper would result in failing the semester. The students started out by picking a subject and then trying to find books to take notes from. This research paper took up about six weeks of the semester. I feel as a former student of this class that English Composition would help anyone become a better writer.